THE LIFE

YOU'VE
ALWAYS
WANTED

Books by John Ortberg

Everybody's Normal Till You Get to Know Them
If You Want to Walk on Water, You've Got to Get Out of the Boat
The Life You've Always Wanted
Love Beyond Reason

THE

LIFE
YOU'VE
ALWAYS
WANTED

JOHN ORTBERG
WITH STEPHEN AND AMANDA SORENSON

ZONDERVAN™

GRAND RAPIDS, MICHIGAN 49530 USA

WILLOW

Willow Creek Resources

LEADER'S GUIDE | SIX SESSIONS ON SPIRITUAL DISCIPLINES FOR ORDINARY PEOPLE

We want to hear from you. Please send your comments about this book to us
in care of zreview@zondervan.com. Thank you.

ZONDERVAN™

The Life You've Always Wanted Leader's Guide
Copyright © 2004 by John Ortberg

Requests for information should be addressed to:
Zondervan, *Grand Rapids, Michigan 49530*

ISBN-10: 0-310-25587-2
ISBN-13: 978-0-310-25587-1

Interior design by Nancy Wilson

Printed in the United States of America

08 09 10 11 • 12 11 10 9 8 7 6

Contents

Preface

If you have ever been frustrated with the state of your spiritual life. If you've ever wondered why spiritual growth seems to go so slowly. If you've ever wondered if real change is possible. If you've ever felt confused or stuck in your spiritual life—you're my kind of person.

I have struggled (and still do struggle) with those same things. But I have also discovered that it is possible to live the life I've always wanted to live. You see, the Christian gospel insists that the transformation of the human personality really is possible. It is never easy. It is rarely quick. But it is possible. I see it happening in people sometimes—occasionally even in myself.

It happens any time people become intensely serious about learning from Jesus how to arrange their lives. It happens any time people set their focus on learning to live as Jesus would live if he were in their place.

Throughout the centuries, wise people have devoted themselves to following Jesus in this way. This series is an attempt to make some of that wisdom accessible to people who live in a world of freeways, corporate ladders, and X boxes. When you are through, my hope is that you will accept Christ's invitation to live life his way because it truly is the life you've always wanted.

—John Ortberg

How to Use This Guide

This Leader's Guide is divided into six sessions approximately fifty-five minutes in length. Each session corresponds to a video presentation, and sessions are based on the book *The Life You've Always Wanted* by John Ortberg.

Although this guide can be used for individual study, it is designed primarily for group study. It can be used for retreats, in small group studies, as a Sunday school elective, and for training individuals to discover and embrace their unique gifts, to recognize God's calling on their lives, to face their challenges and fears, and to experience the reality of God's power in their lives.

BEFORE THE FIRST SESSION

- Watch the video presentation.
- Obtain the necessary Participant's Guides for all participants.
- Make sure you have the items listed below.

Leader's Necessities
- Leader's Guide
- Bible (Old and New Testaments)
- Television
- Video/DVD player (stand, extension cord, etc.)
- Videotape/DVD for the sessions
- Watch or clock with which to monitor time
- Extra pens or pencils if needed by participants

Participant's Necessities
- Participant's Guide
- Bible (Old and New Testaments)
- Pen or pencil

DIRECTIONS FOR THE LEADER

These directions are enclosed in the shaded boxes and are not meant to be read to participants.

SUPPLEMENTARY MATERIALS

Various quotes and charts provide supplementary information that will enhance and deepen participants' understanding of the themes of the sessions. This material is not required reading to complete the session. If your group has more time available than the typical one-hour time slot, you may include the supplementary information as part of your session and expand your discussion or study. Otherwise, these quotes and charts are available as additional resources for participants who want to deepen their study on their own.

Throughout the sessions, Suggested Responses follow group-oriented questions for participants. The Suggested Responses provide an inkling of the responses participants may give and guide you in emphasizing key points.

HOW EACH SESSION IS DIVIDED

Each session is divided into six main parts: Before You Lead, Introduction, Video Presentation, Group Discovery, Personal Journey, and Closing Meditation. A brief explanation of each part follows.

1. BEFORE YOU LEAD

Synopsis

Summarizes the material presented in each session.

Key Points of This Session

Highlights the key points on which you will want to focus.

Suggested Reading

Links each session to the related material in the book *The Life You've Always Wanted* by John Ortberg.

Session Outline

Provides an overview of the content, activities, and time frame.

2. INTRODUCTION

Welcome

Welcomes participants to the session.

What's to Come

A brief, introductory summary you may choose to use.

Questions to Think About

Designed to help you guide participants in thinking about the theme or themes that will be covered. A corresponding page is included in the Participant's Guide.

3. VIDEO PRESENTATION

During this time, you and the participants will watch the video and take notes. Some key themes have been highlighted.

4. GROUP DISCOVERY

In this section, you will guide participants in thinking through the key themes and information presented in each session. You may want to use the material in the order in which it is presented, but feel free to amplify various points with your own material and/or illustrations.

The Leader's Guide includes copies of the corresponding pages in the Participant's Guide. Space is also provided in which to write additional planning notes. Having the Participant's Guide pages in front of you allows you to view the pages the participants are seeing as you talk without having to hold two books at the same time. It also lets you know where the participants are in their book when someone asks you a question.

Video Highlights

Use these questions with the entire group. This will guide participants in verbally responding to key points and themes covered in the video. Some groups will discuss questions more freely and extensively than others. Questions are provided to keep discussion moving within less expressive groups. If you are leading an expressive group and find that you cannot complete as many questions as are provided, pre-select key questions for your group to explore.

Large Group Exploration

During this time, you will guide the group in exploring a theme or topic related to the session. Often a few introductory sentences are provided that set the stage for discussion. Various approaches are used to stimulate learning and discussion. Sometimes questions are offered. Other times, participants will complete charts or discuss Bible passages.

Small Group Exploration

At this time, if your group has more than seven participants, you will break the group into smaller groups (three to five people). Participants will use their Bibles and write down and discuss their responses to the questions. If time allows, representatives of the small groups can share with the entire group the key ideas their group discussed.

Group Discussion

Bring the entire group together to discuss additional questions that wrap up the session. As time allows, feel free to use the material as it is—or adapt it to the needs of your group.

5. PERSONAL JOURNEY

During this time, participants will have the opportunity to consider what they've just discovered and how it applies to their daily lives. Since this is a private, meditative exercise, participants should not talk among themselves. Participants also have the opportunity to continue their journey on their own by completing the "To Do on Your Own" portion.

6. CLOSING MEDITATION

You may close each session with the prayer provided, or use a different prayer.

TIPS FOR LEADING AND PROMOTING GROUP DISCUSSION

1. Allow group members to participate at their own comfort level. Not everyone needs to answer every question. It may take some participants a while to feel comfortable enough to share.

2. Ask questions with interest and warmth, then listen carefully to individual responses. Remember: it is important for participants to think through the questions and ideas presented as part of the process. The *process* is more important than specific answers, which is why *suggested* responses are provided.

3. Be flexible. Reword questions if you wish. Choose to spend more or less time and add or delete questions to accommodate the needs and time frame of your group.

4. Suggest that participants take time to explore any supplementary material that time did not permit them to explore within a session—and review previous sessions. This review will be particularly helpful if each session is being done weekly, for example, rather than all six sessions being done in a retreat setting.

5. Allow for (and expect) differences of opinion and experience.

6. Do not allow any individual(s) to monopolize discussion. If such a situation arises, guide the discussion toward other people and perhaps speak to the person afterward about the importance of allowing everyone to share.

7. If a heated discussion begins on a theological topic, suggest that the participants involved continue their discussion with you after the session is over.

8. If you have time, read *The Life You've Always Wanted* before or in conjunction with these sessions. Obviously not everything in the book could be included in these sessions. Reading the book will provide background that will help you in leading the discussions.

9. Monitor the time frames without being heavy-handed. Although it's important to keep each session moving, remember that the needs of your group may cause you to spend more or less time on a particular part of a session. Also, keep in mind that the content of each session has been designed to enable participants to cover all of the intended material.

10. If time allows, invite participants to talk with you before or after the sessions about what they are learning and thinking. What an encouragement you can be to them—by listening, sharing ideas, sharing your experiences, etc.

11. Approach these sessions with a joyful heart. Many people have benefited from the opportunity to deepen their relationship with God and others as a result of having read *The Life You've Always Wanted*.

12. Do not be afraid of silence. Allow people time to think—don't panic. Sometimes ten seconds of silence seems like an eternity. Remember, some of this material requires time to process—so give people time to digest a question and *then* respond.

13. Last, but certainly not least, ask people to pray for you and your group as you go through these sessions. God wants to do great things in your lives!

It's "Morphing" Time

BEFORE YOU LEAD
Synopsis

God has created each of us to be his masterpiece. Yet when we honestly reflect on who we are, we realize that no matter what we've accomplished we can't escape the nagging feeling that something is missing, that something is not quite as it should be. We bear a sense of disappointment in who we are, what we've done, how we've done it, or what we haven't done. We realize we could be better husbands, wives, friends, and neighbors. We realize that we love God too little and sin too much.

When we realize that we fall short of being who God had in mind when he created us, we are prone to echo the cartoon character Popeye's wistful assessment of inadequacy: "I yam what I yam, and that's all that I yam." This is the sad cry of the human race.

But there is good news. The fallen state in which we now live isn't all there is. The Christian gospel proclaims that God is in the business of transforming ordinary people like us so we can express his character and goodness in our whole being. In fact, the primary goal of spiritual life is authentic human transformation—real change in the essential nature of the person.

This transformation of the human personality involves learning to think as Jesus would think, to feel what he'd feel, to perceive what he'd perceive, and, therefore, to do what he would do. It happens whenever we become intensely serious about learning from Jesus how to arrange our lives.

However, caution is in order. Not all spiritual change is authentic. If we don't let God change us from the inside out, we are tempted to adhere to external rules, behaviors, and/or practices that are intended primarily to identify us to others as "transformed" people. John Ortberg calls this "pseudo-transformation." This misunderstanding of true spirituality has caused immense damage to the human race. It leads people to think they are becoming more spiritual when, in fact, they are becoming more smug and judgmental.

Spiritual transformation is not a matter of trying harder, but of training wisely. Trying can only take us so far. If we are serious about spiritual transformation, we must train for it just as we must train for running a marathon or being a concert pianist. Training involves practicing spiritual disciplines, which can be any activity that opens us up to God's transforming power and helps us live life as Jesus taught and modeled it. These practices help us grow in the ability to do what we cannot do by willpower alone. So it's morphing time—time to learn from God how to live life as Jesus taught and modeled it.

Key Points of This Session

1. *We aren't who we want to be; our hope is to be transformed.* God created us to be his masterpieces, yet we fall short, loving God too little and sin too much. Caught between disappointment and hope, we long to be the works of art God had in mind when he created us. We long to live the life he appointed us to live. Our hope is that the fallen state in which we now live isn't all there is. We long to be transformed, and the Christian gospel insists that such transformation really is possible.

2. *The primary goal of spiritual life is human transformation—real change in the essential nature of the person.* God is in the business of transforming ordinary people like us so that we express his character and goodness in our whole being. This is real transformation from the inside out—learning to think as Jesus would think, to feel what he'd feel, to perceive what he'd perceive, and therefore to do what he would do. It is a far cry from pseudo-transformation, the adherence to external rules or behaviors intended to identify us to others as "transformed" people.

3. *If we are serious about spiritual transformation, we must not merely "try harder," we must "train wisely."* Growth in our relationship with God results from training in the spiritual disciplines. It happens whenever we become intensely serious about learning from Jesus how to arrange our lives. Spiritual disciplines are the practices we live by that enable us to do what we cannot do by willpower alone. These practices help us grow in the ability to love God and people—the true indicators of spiritual well-being.

Suggested Reading

Chapters one, two, and three of *The Life You've Always Wanted*

SESSION OUTLINE

55 MINUTES

    I. Introduction (6 minutes)
       Welcome
       What's to Come
       Questions to Think About

    II. Video Presentation: "It's 'Morphing' Time" (13 minutes)

    III. Group Discovery (29 minutes)
       Video Highlights (5 minutes)
       Large Group Exploration (11 minutes)
       Small Group Exploration (8 minutes)
       Group Discussion (5 minutes)

    IV. Personal Journey (6 minutes)

    V. Closing Meditation (1 minute)

The good news as Jesus preached it is that now it is possible for ordinary men and women to live in the presence and under the power of God. . . . It is not about the minimal entrance requirements for getting into heaven when you die. It is about the glorious redemption of human life — your life. It's morphing time.

—John Ortberg

It's "Morphing" Time

INTRODUCTION

⟨ **6** MINUTES ⟩

Welcome

> Participant's Guide page 9.
>
> Welcome participants to *The Life You've Always Wanted* session one, "It's 'Morphing' Time."

What's to Come

God has created each of us to be his masterpiece, yet not one of us is fully satisfied. No matter what we've accomplished, we each bear a sense of disappointment in who we are, what we've done, how we've done it, or what we haven't done. We can't escape the nagging realization that something is missing, that all is not quite as it should be.

And the truth is, our human condition isn't what it should be. We long to be all that we can be but have failed to be the people God created us to be. Consequently, we are missing out on the life he intended us to live.

But there is good news: the fallen state in which we now live isn't all there is. The Christian gospel insists that the transformation of the human personality really is possible. It happens whenever we become intensely serious about learning from Jesus how to arrange

It's "Morphing" Time

SESSION ONE

The good news as Jesus preached it is that now it is possible for ordinary men and women to live in the presence and under the power of God. . . . It is not about the minimal entrance requirements for getting into heaven when you die. It is about the glorious redemption of human life—your life. It's morphing time.

—John Ortberg

9

PLANNING NOTES

our lives. So we're going to explore what spiritual transformation is about and discover how we can open ourselves up to be transformed by God.

Let's begin by considering a few questions related to spiritual transformation. These questions are on page 10 of your Participant's Guide.

Questions to Think About

> Participant's Guide page 10.
>
> As time permits, ask participants to respond to two or more of the following questions.

1. To be *transformed* means to be changed, and transformation is taking place all around us all the time. What examples of transformation—of any sort—come to mind?

This open-ended question will help participants realize that transformation means to be changed and that change occurs constantly. Everyday examples of transformation might include: the renovation of a run-down factory into a beautiful office complex; the change that takes place in a small lakeside town that becomes a resort destination; the change in physique and confidence of a skinny boy as he grows into a competitive athlete; the sparkling, magical beauty of a bleak winter landscape blanketed by deep snow; the restoration of a classic car. Of course transformation can be equally dramatic on the negative side: the beachfront after a severe hurricane, or a riverbank community after a major flood; the destruction of a beautiful city during wartime; the once-strong but withered body of a drug addict or alcoholic. All of these are examples of transformation.

2. What is required for transformations such as those you have mentioned to occur?

It is important that participants realize that transformation doesn't happen on its own or by accident. In order for something to be transformed, force must be applied or action must be taken. Transformation is the result of deliberate (and often sustained) effort. Spiritual transformation is the result of training.

Positive
- Our bodies - exercise
- Our church

Negative
- Our bodies as we age
- Disaster damage

QUESTIONS TO THINK ABOUT

1. To be *transformed* means to be changed, and transformation is taking place all around us all the time. What examples of transformation—of any sort—come to mind?

2. What is required for transformations such as those you have mentioned to occur?

3. Although we use the term *spiritual transformation*, we often use it casually without giving it much thought. Describe what *spiritual transformation* means to you.

4. What do you consider to be the indicators of spiritual transformation? How can we tell if another person has experienced a spiritual transformation?

PLANNING NOTES

3. Although we use the term *spiritual transformation,* we often use it casually without giving it much thought. Describe what *spiritual transformation* means to you.

   Allow participants to describe what they think spiritual transformation is. Some may describe it in terms of following biblical commands, others in terms of specific outward behaviors, and others in terms of changed attitudes.

4. What do you consider to be the indicators of spiritual transformation? How can we tell if another person has experienced a spiritual transformation?

   Expect some interesting discussion on this one! Some Christians use external, superficial indicators to show that they are spiritually changed people. These may include not smoking cigarettes, not wearing certain clothing, not listening to certain kinds of music, going to church services often, staying away from certain types of "sinners," etc. Others may focus on "doing good," spending time in Bible study, or giving time and money to the church as indicators of spiritual transformation. Still others may point out that spiritual transformation is an internal process that can't be fully discerned through external behavior.

Let's keep these ideas in mind as we view the video. There is space to take notes on page 11 of your Participant's Guide.

10 • The Life You've Always Wanted Participant's Guide

QUESTIONS TO THINK ABOUT

1. To be *transformed* means to be changed, and transformation is taking place all around us all the time. What examples of transformation—of any sort—come to mind?

2. What is required for transformations such as those you have mentioned to occur?

3. Although we use the term *spiritual transformation*, we often use it casually without giving it much thought. Describe what *spiritual transformation* means to you.

4. What do you consider to be the indicators of spiritual transformation? How can we tell if another person has experienced a spiritual transformation?

Session One: It's "Morphing" Time • 11

VIDEO OBSERVATIONS

Life: disappointment and hope

We shall "morph" indeed

Pseudo-transformation

Trying harder versus training wisely

PLANNING NOTES

VIDEO PRESENTATION: "IT'S 'MORPHING' TIME"

〈 **13** MINUTES 〉

Participant's Guide page 11.

Video Observations

Life: disappointment and hope

We shall "morph" indeed

Pseudo-transformation

Trying harder versus training wisely

GROUP DISCOVERY

〈 **29** MINUTES 〉

If your group has seven or more members, use the Video Highlights with the entire group (5 minutes), then complete the Large Group Exploration (11 minutes), and break into small groups of three to five people for the Small Group Exploration (8 minutes). At the end, bring everyone together for the closing Group Discussion (5 minutes).

If your group has fewer than seven members, begin with the Video Highlights (5 minutes), then complete both the Large Group Exploration (11 minutes) and the Small Group Exploration (8 minutes). Wrap up your discovery time with the Group Discussion (5 minutes).

Please turn to page 12 of your Participant's Guide.

VIDEO OBSERVATIONS

Life: disappointment and hope

We shall "morph" indeed

Pseudo-transformation

Trying harder versus training wisely

VIDEO HIGHLIGHTS

1. What is the hope of the Christian gospel as John Ortberg describes it?

2. An important concept in *The Life You've Always Wanted* is that we are always being transformed; we are always changing for better or for worse. This happens physically and, although it's less obvious, spiritually. How might some of our daily practices cause us to be "formed" spiritually in one direction or another?

3. Why did Jesus so strongly challenge pseudo-transformation and the rabbis' "boundary markers" regarding dietary laws, the Sabbath, and circumcision?

4. In what ways does pseudo-transformation creep into churches today, and what are its damaging effects? Can you identify any "boundary markers" in your church?

PLANNING NOTES

Video Highlights • *5 minutes*

> Participant's Guide page 12.
>
> As time permits, ask one or more of the following questions, which directly relate to the video the participants have just seen.

1. What is the hope of the Christian gospel as John Ortberg describes it?

   SUGGESTED RESPONSE: *The hope of the gospel is much more than just getting into heaven when we die. Jesus came to earth so that we might have an abundant life here and now. We all long for such a life, but on our own it is always beyond our reach. The Christian gospel insists that authentic spiritual transformation really is possible. We can genuinely grow in love, peace, and joy when we are being transformed by God.*

2. An important concept in *The Life You've Always Wanted* is that we are always being transformed; we are always changing for better or for worse. This happens physically and, although it's less obvious, spiritually. How might some of our daily practices cause us to be "formed" spiritually in one direction or another?

   SUGGESTED RESPONSE: *Similar to the way in which our daily health habits—what and how much we eat, how much we exercise—form us in a particular direction physically, our daily spiritual habits form us as well. Obviously the traditional spiritual disciplines of prayer, Bible study, meditation, solitude, and the like can be part of the spiritual transformation process. Choosing to approach life in accordance with the fruit of the Spirit also can move us toward positive spiritual transformation. Seeking to bring every thought "captive" to Christ can be another way to be "formed" in the likeness of Jesus. In the negative sense, overlooking or minimizing what we consider to be "little" sins can form us as well. Focusing our minds on the concerns of life—food, shelter, wealth, power—as opposed to the concerns of God's kingdom can also shape us spiritually.*

12 • The Life You've Always Wanted Participant's Guide

VIDEO HIGHLIGHTS

1. What is the hope of the Christian gospel as John Ortberg describes it?

2. An important concept in *The Life You've Always Wanted* is that we are always being transformed; we are always changing for better or for worse. This happens physically and, although it's less obvious, spiritually. How might some of our daily practices cause us to be "formed" spiritually in one direction or another?

3. Why did Jesus so strongly challenge pseudo-transformation and the rabbis' "boundary markers" regarding dietary laws, the Sabbath, and circumcision?

4. In what ways does pseudo-transformation creep into churches today, and what are its damaging effects? Can you identify any "boundary markers" in your church?

PLANNING NOTES

Loving sin too much and God too little

God:
Like an enormous fairy tale, but it's true

Authentic transformation
The legalistic or visual "look" that ~~does~~ doesn't really mean you are spiritually transformed.

3. Why did Jesus so strongly challenge pseudo-transformation and the rabbis' "boundary markers" regarding dietary laws, the Sabbath, and circumcision?

   SUGGESTED RESPONSE: *Jesus was concerned about authentic spiritual transformation—the condition of the heart—not superficial boundary markers. He wanted people to experience God's transforming power, not just embrace ways to set themselves apart from other people so they could feel good about themselves.*

4. In what ways does pseudo-transformation creep into churches today, and what are its damaging effects? Can you identify any "boundary markers" in your church?

   SUGGESTED RESPONSE: *Rather than experiencing authentic transformation—focusing on loving God and other people—some people create "boundary markers" to position themselves as "insiders" set apart from people who are "outside." They use dress, vocabulary, knowledge, and/or behavior to define themselves as spiritual people. As a result, people who don't conform to these requirements are judged as being less spiritual or are excluded from the accepted group. There is little or no joy in such an environment, and non-Christians are not drawn to the gospel.*

Please turn to page 13 of your Participant's Guide, and we will further explore the path of authentic transformation.

Large Group Exploration • 11 minutes

> Participant's Guide page 13.

Pseudo-Transformation vs. Morphing

When our lives are not marked by genuine, God-directed spiritual change, we tend to look for substitute ways to distinguish ourselves from those we consider to be less spiritual. We adopt boundary markers—highly visible, relatively superficial practices intended to quickly separate the "insiders" from the "outsiders." These boundary markers may include conformity to specified forms of dress and speech, adherence to certain rules of behavior, participation in

VIDEO HIGHLIGHTS

1. What is the hope of the Christian gospel as John Ortberg describes it?

2. An important concept in *The Life You've Always Wanted* is that we are always being transformed; we are always changing for better or for worse. This happens physically and, although it's less obvious, spiritually. How might some of our daily practices cause us to be "formed" spiritually in one direction or another?

3. Why did Jesus so strongly challenge pseudo-transformation and the rabbis' "boundary markers" regarding dietary laws, the Sabbath, and circumcision?

4. In what ways does pseudo-transformation creep into churches today, and what are its damaging effects? Can you identify any "boundary markers" in your church?

LARGE GROUP EXPLORATION

Pseudo-Transformation vs. Morphing

When our lives are not marked by genuine, God-directed spiritual change, we tend to look for substitute ways to distinguish ourselves from those we consider to be less spiritual. We adopt boundary markers—highly visible, relatively superficial practices intended to quickly separate the "insiders" from the "outsiders." These boundary markers may include conformity to specified forms of dress and speech, adherence to certain rules of behavior, participation in prescribed activities, and so on. They provide a false sense of security and superiority.

The religious leaders of Jesus' day focused a great deal of their attention on boundary markers. Many of their conflicts with Jesus occurred because Jesus took a radically different approach to assessing spirituality. Instead of focusing on visible indicators of spiritual transformation, Jesus focused on what was happening in the heart. His concern was whether or not people were being transformed and growing in their love of God and love of people. His concern was whether or not they were "morphing" into the masterpieces God created them to be.

Let's consider these opposing perspectives on spiritual transformation.

1. Read Matthew 12:1–2; 15:1–2; Luke 18:11–12. Note the types of spiritual behaviors the religious leaders of Jesus' day considered important. What was Jesus' assessment of their spirituality? (See Mark 7:5–8.)

PLANNING NOTES

prescribed activities, and so on. They provide a false sense of security and superiority.

The religious leaders of Jesus' day focused a great deal of their attention on boundary markers. Many of their conflicts with Jesus occurred because Jesus took a radically different approach to assessing spirituality. Instead of focusing on visible indicators of spiritual transformation, Jesus focused on what was happening in the heart. His concern was whether or not people were being transformed and growing in their love of God and love of people. His concern was whether or not they were "morphing" into the masterpieces God created them to be.

Let's consider these opposing perspectives on spiritual transformation.

1. Read Matthew 12:1–2; 15:1–2; Luke 18:11–12. Note the types of spiritual behaviors the religious leaders of Jesus' day considered important. What was Jesus' assessment of their spirituality? (See Mark 7:5–8.)

   SUGGESTED RESPONSE: *The religious leaders were consumed by their religious practices—obeying Sabbath laws, washing their hands before they ate, fasting, tithing, and observing rules that set them apart as "better" than other people. Jesus called them hypocrites because they worked hard to communicate the right image by honoring God with their lips, but their hearts were far from him. He accused them of rejecting God's commands and holding on to the teachings of men, and declared their worship to be in vain.*

2. What did Jesus say that no doubt shocked the religious leaders? (Read Matthew 21:28–32.)

   SUGGESTED RESPONSE: *Jesus told the leaders (who were proud of their self-appointed spiritual status) that tax collectors and prostitutes (who the leaders considered to be "outsiders") were entering the kingdom of God ahead of them! He emphasized that righteousness resulted from a real change of heart—a change they had rejected.*

LARGE GROUP EXPLORATION

Pseudo-Transformation vs. Morphing

When our lives are not marked by genuine, God-directed spiritual change, we tend to look for substitute ways to distinguish ourselves from those we consider to be less spiritual. We adopt boundary markers—highly visible, relatively superficial practices intended to quickly separate the "insiders" from the "outsiders." These boundary markers may include conformity to specified forms of dress and speech, adherence to certain rules of behavior, participation in prescribed activities, and so on. They provide a false sense of security and superiority.

The religious leaders of Jesus' day focused a great deal of their attention on boundary markers. Many of their conflicts with Jesus occurred because Jesus took a radically different approach to assessing spirituality. Instead of focusing on visible indicators of spiritual transformation, Jesus focused on what was happening in the heart. His concern was whether or not people were being transformed and growing in their love of God and love of people. His concern was whether or not they were "morphing" into the masterpieces God created them to be.

Let's consider these opposing perspectives on spiritual transformation.

1. Read Matthew 12:1–2; 15:1–2; Luke 18:11–12. Note the types of spiritual behaviors the religious leaders of Jesus' day considered important. What was Jesus' assessment of their spirituality? (See Mark 7:5–8.)

2. What did Jesus say that no doubt shocked the religious leaders? (Read Matthew 21:28–32.)

3. Instead of focusing on external religious practices, what did Jesus emphasize? (Read Luke 10:25–28; John 13:34–35.)

4. What is the evidence of true spiritual transformation in our lives? (Read 1 Corinthians 13:1–7.)

5. Now let's consider "morphing." The word *morph* comes from the Greek word *morphoo*, which means "the inward and real formation of the essential nature of a person." The term was used to describe the formation and growth of an embryo in a mother's body.

   The kind of spiritual transformation God wants each of us to experience is a complete "remaking" of our nature. He wants us to see, feel, think, and do what Jesus would if he were in our unique place. What makes such a transformation possible, and why is it important? (See Romans 6:3–14; 2 Corinthians 5:17–20; Ephesians 2:10.)

PLANNING NOTES

3. Instead of focusing on external religious practices, what did Jesus emphasize? (Read Luke 10:25–28; John 13:34–35.)

SUGGESTED RESPONSE: *Jesus said that the way to have life is to love God and love your neighbor, and that love (not rules and external "boundary markers") would be the identifying mark of his disciples.*

4. What is the evidence of true spiritual transformation in our lives? (Read 1 Corinthians 13:1–7.)

SUGGESTED RESPONSE: *Paul makes it clear that no matter what great, "spiritual" things we can do, they amount to nothing if they come from a heart that is not transformed by love. We can talk about God, understand all knowledge, have great faith, sacrifice to help needy people, and even become martyrs, but if we don't have love we gain nothing. If we are growing in our love for God and other people, our love will be patient, kind, and forgiving, not envious, proud, rude, self-seeking, or easily angered. Such love rejoices with the truth, always protecting, trusting, hoping, and persevering.*

5. Now let's consider "morphing." The word *morph* comes from the Greek word *morphoo*, which means "the inward and real formation of the essential nature of a person." The term was used to describe the formation and growth of an embryo in a mother's body.

   The kind of spiritual transformation God wants each of us to experience is a complete "remaking" of our nature. He wants us to see, feel, think, and do what Jesus would if he were in our unique place. What makes such a transformation possible, and why is it important? (See Romans 6:3–14; 2 Corinthians 5:17–20; Ephesians 2:10.)

SUGGESTED RESPONSE: *When we accept God's gift of salvation and choose to unite ourselves with Christ, we become new creatures. Because of Christ's death and resurrection, we are reconciled to God—dead to sin and alive to Christ. Sin no longer has mastery over us, so we need to offer ourselves to God to be his "instruments" and "ambassadors" of righteousness. That's quite a transformation! It is important because we are God's masterpieces, created in Jesus to do the good works God has prepared for us to do.*

14 • The Life You've Always Wanted Participant's Guide

2. What did Jesus say that no doubt shocked the religious leaders? (Read Matthew 21:28–32.)

3. Instead of focusing on external religious practices, what did Jesus emphasize? (Read Luke 10:25–28; John 13:34–35.)

4. What is the evidence of true spiritual transformation in our lives? (Read 1 Corinthians 13:1–7.)

5. Now let's consider "morphing." The word *morph* comes from the Greek word *morphoo,* which means "the inward and real formation of the essential nature of a person." The term was used to describe the formation and growth of an embryo in a mother's body.

   The kind of spiritual transformation God wants each of us to experience is a complete "remaking" of our nature. He wants us to see, feel, think, and do what Jesus would if he were in our unique place. What makes such a transformation possible, and why is it important? (See Romans 6:3–14; 2 Corinthians 5:17–20; Ephesians 2:10.)

PLANNING NOTES

6. Another form of the word *morph* is used in the phrase "until Christ is formed in you" in Galatians 4:19. This word, *summorphizo,* means "to have the same form as another, to shape a thing into a durable likeness."

   Our spiritual growth is to be a molding process, a process whereby we are shaped in the image of Christ. Notice what the following verses reveal about the process of spiritual growth God accomplishes within each Christian.

   a. Galatians 4:19

      SUGGESTED RESPONSE: *This process is so important that the apostle Paul agonized over the people of Galatia until Christ was born in them and they expressed Christ's character and goodness in their whole being.*

   b. Colossians 3:5–10

      SUGGESTED RESPONSE: *We can't be formed into a new likeness if we hang on to the old mold. We need to deliberately put off our old ways and allow our new self to be shaped by our Creator's hand.*

   c. 2 Corinthians 3:18

      SUGGESTED RESPONSE: *As we are increasingly transformed into God's likeness, we reflect ever-increasing amounts of his glory to the world around us.*

7. In Romans 12:2, Paul used the word *metamorphoo,* from which we get the English word *metamorphosis.* The emphasis is that we don't simply learn to *do* things in a new way, we *become* the kind of people who *are* that way. How does this transformation come about?

   SUGGESTED RESPONSE: *We become new creatures because God is at work in us, changing us by renewing our minds, by changing who we are and our motivation for doing what we do.*

6. Another form of the word *morph* is used in the phrase "until Christ is formed in you" in Galatians 4:19. This word, *summorphizo*, means "to have the same form as another, to shape a thing into a durable likeness."

Our spiritual growth is to be a molding process, a process whereby we are shaped in the image of Christ. Notice what the following verses reveal about the process of spiritual growth God accomplishes within each Christian.

a. Galatians 4:19

b. Colossians 3:5–10

c. 2 Corinthians 3:18

7. In Romans 12:2, Paul used the word *metamorphoo,* from which we get the English word *metamorphosis.* The emphasis is that we don't simply learn to *do* things in a new way, we *become* the kind of people who *are* that way. How does this transformation come about?

PLANNING NOTES

The Impact of Pseudo-Transformation

We might be tempted to wonder if morphing makes any practical, daily-life differences as opposed to pseudo-transformation. Consider the perspective author Sheldon Vanauken offers in his critically acclaimed book *A Severe Mercy:* The strongest argument for Christianity is Christians, when they are drawing life from God. The strongest argument against Christianity? Also Christians, when they become exclusive, self-righteous, and complacent.

Consider, too, the warning signs of pseudo-transformation that appear in Matthew 23, where Jesus denounced the religious leaders of his day for their lack of true spiritual life. As you identify these warning signs, think about the ways these signs show up among Christians today.

Matthew 23	Warning Signs of Pseudo-Transformation
Verses 1–4	Demanding obedience from others, but not practicing what they preach; burdening other people with the pursuit of exhaustive, external rules and practices yet not helping to bear the burden.
Verses 5–8	Doing their spiritual duties so that other people will notice and honor them; expecting others to honor them; taking pride in their knowledge, position, and influence.
Verses 13–15	Making it difficult for other people to enter (and in some cases preventing people from entering) God's kingdom; refusing to enter the kingdom of heaven themselves.
Verse 23	Following the letter of the law but violating the spirit of the law such as by tithing every little thing to God, yet neglecting justice, mercy, and faithfulness.
Verses 24–29	Preoccupied with *appearing* to be spiritual; cleaning up the outside, but doing nothing to clean the mess on the inside; being hypocritical.

We will now break into groups of three to five to complete the Small Group Exploration, which begins on page 17. I will give you a one-minute notice before we rejoin for our Group Discussion.

Small Group Exploration • 8 minutes

Participant's Guide page 17.

Training for Spiritual Growth

We all know that training is necessary if we want to succeed in physical competition. It is also true that training is necessary if we are serious about growing in our relationship with God. Learning to

16 • The Life You've Always Wanted Participant's Guide

The Impact of Pseudo-Transformation

We might be tempted to wonder if morphing makes any practical, daily-life differences as opposed to pseudo-transformation. Consider the perspective author Sheldon Vanauken offers in his critically acclaimed book *A Severe Mercy*: the strongest argument for Christianity is Christians, when they are drawing life from God. The strongest argument against Christianity? Also Christians, when they become exclusive, self-righteous, and complacent.

Consider, too, the warning signs of pseudo-transformation that appear in Matthew 23, where Jesus denounced the religious leaders of his day for their lack of true spiritual life. As you identify these warning signs, think about the ways these signs show up among Christians today.

Matthew 23	Warning Signs of Pseudo-Transformation
Verses 1–4	Demanding obedience from others, but not practicing what they preach; burdening other people with the pursuit of exhaustive, external rules and practices yet not helping to bear the burden.
Verses 5–8	Doing their spiritual duties so that other people will notice and honor them; expecting others to honor them; taking pride in their knowledge, position, and influence.
Verses 13–15	Making it difficult for other people to enter (and in some cases preventing people from entering) God's kingdom; refusing to enter the kingdom of heaven themselves.
Verse 23	Following the letter of the law but violating the spirit of the law such as by tithing every little thing to God, yet neglecting justice, mercy, and faithfulness.
Verses 24–29	Preoccupied with *appearing* to be spiritual; cleaning up the outside, but doing nothing to clean the mess on the inside; being hypocritical.

Session One: It's "Morphing" Time • 17

SMALL GROUP EXPLORATION

Training for Spiritual Growth

We all know that training is necessary if we want to succeed in physical competition. It is also true that training is necessary if we are serious about growing in our relationship with God. Learning to think, feel, and act like Jesus is at least as demanding as learning to run a marathon or play the piano. We can't succeed simply by trying hard. We can't succeed on willpower alone. We need to prepare ourselves to receive God's transforming work within us. We need to train wisely.

1. When the apostle Paul wrote about training to run a race (1 Corinthians 9:24–27), he and his readers knew exactly what he was talking about. Corinth was the site of the Isthmian Games, second only to the Olympics in prominence in ancient Greece. Paul probably visited Corinth during the games of AD 51 and may have made tents for the visitors and contestants. What is the spiritual "prize" for which Paul ran, and why did he take spiritual training so seriously? (See 1 Corinthians 9:25–27.)

2. What did Paul encourage his young protégé, Timothy, to do? Why? (See 1 Timothy 4:7–8.)

PLANNING NOTES

think, feel, and act like Jesus is at least as demanding as learning to run a marathon or play the piano. We can't succeed simply by trying hard. We can't succeed on willpower alone. We need to prepare ourselves to receive God's transforming work within us. We need to train wisely.

1. When the apostle Paul wrote about training to run a race (1 Corinthians 9:24–27), he and his readers knew exactly what he was talking about. Corinth was the site of the Isthmian Games, second only to the Olympics in prominence in ancient Greece. Paul probably visited Corinth during the games of AD 51 and may have made tents for the visitors and contestants. What is the spiritual "prize" for which Paul ran, and why did he take spiritual training so seriously? (See 1 Corinthians 9:25–27.)

   SUGGESTED RESPONSE: *Paul ran for the "crown" of eternal life. He trained diligently because he didn't want to be disqualified—especially after he'd preached the gospel to others.*

2. What did Paul encourage his young protégé, Timothy, to do? Why? (See 1 Timothy 4:7–8.)

   SUGGESTED RESPONSE: *He urged Timothy to take his faith seriously and to train himself "to be godly" because godliness has value for life on earth as well as for eternal life.*

3. We may think that following Jesus and growing spiritually come about automatically and easily rather than through dedicated training, but that is not what Jesus taught. Read Mark 8:34–35 and Luke 14:27–30, 33. Notice what Jesus told the crowds that followed him about the path of spiritual growth.

   SUGGESTED RESPONSE: *Jesus emphasized that following him is a sacrificial choice—a choice that is both costly and life-giving. He urged them to count the cost of discipleship carefully.*

4. We need to train ourselves for spiritual growth, but there's a big difference between fist-clenching, teeth-gritting exertion to become "more spiritual" and the transformed life Jesus offers. The following passages are essential to our understanding of how training for authentic spiritual transformation works.

SMALL GROUP EXPLORATION

Training for Spiritual Growth

We all know that training is necessary if we want to succeed in physical competition. It is also true that training is necessary if we are serious about growing in our relationship with God. Learning to think, feel, and act like Jesus is at least as demanding as learning to run a marathon or play the piano. We can't succeed simply by trying hard. We can't succeed on willpower alone. We need to prepare ourselves to receive God's transforming work within us. We need to train wisely.

1. When the apostle Paul wrote about training to run a race (1 Corinthians 9:24–27), he and his readers knew exactly what he was talking about. Corinth was the site of the Isthmian Games, second only to the Olympics in prominence in ancient Greece. Paul probably visited Corinth during the games of AD 51 and may have made tents for the visitors and contestants. What is the spiritual "prize" for which Paul ran, and why did he take spiritual training so seriously? (See 1 Corinthians 9:25–27.)

2. What did Paul encourage his young protégé, Timothy, to do? Why? (See 1 Timothy 4:7–8.)

3. We may think that following Jesus and growing spiritually come about automatically and easily rather than through dedicated training, but that is not what Jesus taught. Read Mark 8:34–35 and Luke 14:27–30, 33. Notice what Jesus told the crowds that followed him about the path of spiritual growth.

4. We need to train ourselves for spiritual growth, but there's a big difference between fist-clenching, teeth-gritting exertion to become "more spiritual" and the transformed life Jesus offers. The following passages are essential to our understanding of how training for authentic spiritual transformation works.

   a. Read Matthew 11:28–30 and Romans 8:11. Notice how pursuing the life Jesus offers differs from the demands of pseudo-transformation.

   b. What do we learn about our ability to pursue spiritual growth from 2 Corinthians 12:9–10 and Philippians 4:13?

PLANNING NOTES

a. Read Matthew 11:28–30 and Romans 8:11. Notice how pursuing the life Jesus offers differs from the demands of pseudo-transformation.

SUGGESTED RESPONSE: *Although following Jesus requires training, his teaching (his "yoke") is not burdensome. Jesus offers rest for those who are weary and burdened. He does not abandon us in our pursuit of spiritual growth. Instead, the Holy Spirit lives and works within every Christian, bringing us life.*

b. What do we learn about our ability to pursue spiritual growth from 2 Corinthians 12:9–10 and Philippians 4:13?

SUGGESTED RESPONSE: *The transformed life Jesus offers is not only for the strong or powerful. It is available to everyone who pursues it, no matter how weak or infirm. When we are weak, God shows himself to be strong. In the strength of God's power—the same power that raised Jesus from the dead—we can accomplish everything he calls us to do.*

c. What encouragement does 2 Thessalonians 2:16–17 offer us?

SUGGESTED RESPONSE: *God loves us and gives us hope. He encourages and strengthens us "in every good deed and word."*

5. To what did Jesus compare the possibility of living in the kingdom of God—of living the life you've always wanted? (See Matthew 13:44–46.)

SUGGESTED RESPONSE: *Jesus compared it to a treasure that is worth sacrificing everything we have to obtain.*

> Let participants know when one minute remains.
>
> When time is up, ask the groups to rejoin as one group.

3. We may think that following Jesus and growing spiritually come about automatically and easily rather than through dedicated training, but that is not what Jesus taught. Read Mark 8:34–35 and Luke 14:27–30, 33. Notice what Jesus told the crowds that followed him about the path of spiritual growth.

4. We need to train ourselves for spiritual growth, but there's a big difference between fist-clenching, teeth-gritting exertion to become "more spiritual" and the transformed life Jesus offers. The following passages are essential to our understanding of how training for authentic spiritual transformation works.

   a. Read Matthew 11:28–30 and Romans 8:11. Notice how pursuing the life Jesus offers differs from the demands of pseudo-transformation.

   b. What do we learn about our ability to pursue spiritual growth from 2 Corinthians 12:9–10 and Philippians 4:13?

   c. What encouragement does 2 Thessalonians 2:16–17 offer us?

5. To what did Jesus compare the possibility of living in the kingdom of God—of living the life you've always wanted? (See Matthew 13:44–46.)

PLANNING NOTES

Group Discussion • *5 minutes*

> Participant's Guide page 20.
>
> As time permits, discuss the following questions that will help participants explore their understanding of the concepts covered in this session.

Now it's time for us to wrap up our discovery time. Please turn to page 20.

1. Let's talk a bit more about spiritual disciplines. How does John Ortberg's definition of spiritual disciplines differ from how you have thought of them? In what ways does this definition change your behavior or how you approach and what you expect from your spiritual life?

2. Søren Kierkegaard once said, "Now, with God's help, I shall become myself." In what ways is this an accurate representation of authentic spiritual transformation?

3. Why do you think we are prone to substitute pseudo-transformation for authentic transformation? Why is it so easy to fall into the trap of saying or doing things we think spiritual people are supposed to say or do? Of hiding our sin? Of working hard to make people think we're loving instead of actually loving them?

What Is a Spiritual Discipline?

John Ortberg defines a spiritual discipline as any activity that can help us gain power to live life as Jesus taught and modeled it. Spiritual disciplines are a means of appropriating or growing toward the life God graciously offers. They allow us to do what we cannot do by willpower alone. So practices such as reading Scripture and praying are important not because they prove how spiritual we are but because God can use them to lead us into the kingdom life he offers.

GROUP DISCUSSION

1. Let's talk a bit more about spiritual disciplines. How does John Ortberg's definition of spiritual disciplines differ from how you have thought of them? In what ways does this definition change your behavior or how you approach and what you expect from your spiritual life?

What Is a Spiritual Discipline?

John Ortberg defines a spiritual discipline as any activity that can help us gain power to live life as Jesus taught and modeled it. Spiritual disciplines are a means of appropriating or growing toward the life God graciously offers. They allow us to do what we cannot do by willpower alone. So practices such as reading Scripture and praying are important not because they prove how spiritual we are but because God can use them to lead us into the kingdom life he offers.

---

2. Søren Kierkegaard once said, "Now, with God's help, I shall become myself." In what ways is this an accurate representation of authentic spiritual transformation?

3. Why do you think we are prone to substitute pseudo-transformation for authentic transformation? Why is it so easy to fall into the trap of saying or doing things we think spiritual people are supposed to say or do? Of hiding our sin? Of working hard to make people think we're loving instead of actually loving them?

PLANNING NOTES

PERSONAL JOURNEY: TO DO NOW

6 MINUTES

> Participant's Guide page 22.

Now let's turn to page 22 and each spend a few minutes alone with God to review the key points and begin considering how what we've explored today makes a difference in our daily lives.

1. *We aren't who we want to be; our hope is to be transformed.* God created us to be his masterpieces, yet we fall short, loving God too little and sin too much. Caught between disappointment and hope, we long for the life he appointed us to live. Our hope is that our fallen state isn't all there is and that the transformation promised in the Christian gospel really is possible.

   In *The Life You've Always Wanted,* John Ortberg mentioned Popeye the Sailor Man, who said, "I yam what I yam." Popeye seemed sad, aware of his shortcomings and not anticipating much growth or change. Think about your disappointments honestly. In what way(s) have you struggled between disappointment and hope?

   We all face disappointment in ourselves, such as not being the parents we want to be or "loving sin too much and God too little." Which disappointments are most painful to you?

   Describe the spiritual hope to which you look forward.

2. *The primary goal of spiritual life is human transformation—real change in the essential nature of the person.* God is in the business of transforming ordinary people like us so that we express his character and goodness in our whole being. This is real transformation from the inside out—learning to think as Jesus would think, to feel what he'd feel, to perceive what he'd perceive, and therefore to do what he would do. It is a far cry from pseudo-transformation, the adherence to external rules or behaviors intended to identify us to others as "transformed" people.

PERSONAL JOURNEY: TO DO NOW

1. *We aren't who we want to be; our hope is to be transformed.* God created us to be his masterpieces, yet we fall short, loving God too little and sin too much. Caught between disappointment and hope, we long for the life he appointed us to live. Our hope is that our fallen state isn't all there is and that the transformation promised in the Christian gospel really is possible.

   In *The Life You've Always Wanted,* John Ortberg mentioned Popeye the Sailor Man, who said, "I yam what I yam." Popeye seemed sad, aware of his shortcomings and not anticipating much growth or change. Think about your disappointments honestly. In what way(s) have you struggled between disappointment and hope?

   We all face disappointment in ourselves, such as not being the parents we want to be or "loving sin too much and God too little." Which disappointments are most painful to you?

   Describe the spiritual hope to which you look forward.

2. *The primary goal of spiritual life is human transformation—real change in the essential nature of the person.* God is in the business of transforming ordinary people like us so that we express his character and goodness in our whole being. This is real transformation from the inside out—learning to think as Jesus would think, to feel what he'd feel, to perceive what he'd perceive, and therefore to do what he would do. It is a far cry from pseudo-transformation, the adherence to external rules or behaviors intended to identify us to others as "transformed" people.

   If someone asked you, "How is your spiritual life going?" how would you respond? What would you say about yourself that would be impressive? What would you hesitate to reveal?

   What standard do you use to evaluate your spiritual condition?

3. *If we are serious about spiritual transformation, we must not merely "try harder," we must "train wisely."* Growth in our relationship with God results from training in the spiritual disciplines. It happens whenever we become intensely serious about learning from Jesus how to arrange our lives. Spiritual disciplines are the practices we live by that enable us to do what we cannot do by willpower

PLANNING NOTES

If someone asked you, "How is your spiritual life going?" how would you respond? What would you say about yourself that would be impressive? What would you hesitate to reveal?

What standard do you use to evaluate your spiritual condition?

3. *If we are serious about spiritual transformation, we must not merely "try harder," we must "train wisely."* Growth in our relationship with God results from training in the spiritual disciplines. It happens whenever we become intensely serious about learning from Jesus how to arrange our lives. Spiritual disciplines are the practices we live by that enable us to do what we cannot do by willpower alone. These practices help us grow in the ability to love God and people—the true indicators of spiritual well-being.

Would you say that you are *training* to become more like Christ, or *trying* to be more like Christ? Why?

John Ortberg emphasizes that we can't transform ourselves; God transforms us. How would you describe the difference between spiritual training and self-transformation? In what way(s) have you attempted self-transformation?

You will have the opportunity to further develop a personal spiritual training plan as this series progresses. For now, write down a few ideas of what spiritual training might involve for you.

> Let participants know when there is one minute remaining.
>
> When time is up, remind participants that they may want to continue their journey between sessions by completing the Personal Journey exercises on pages 25–27 of their Participant's Guide. Then end the session with the Closing Meditation.

2. *The primary goal of spiritual life is human transformation—real change in the essential nature of the person.* God is in the business of transforming ordinary people like us so that we express his character and goodness in our whole being This is real transformation from the inside out—learning to think as Jesus would think, to feel what he'd feel, to perceive what he'd perceive, and therefore to do what he would do. It is a far cry from pseudo-transformation, the adherence to external rules or behaviors intended to identify us to others as "transformed" people.

If someone asked you, "How is your spiritual life going?" how would you respond? What would you say about yourself that would be impressive? What would you hesitate to reveal?

What standard do you use to evaluate your spiritual condition?

3. *If we are serious about spiritual transformation, we must not merely "try harder," we must "train wisely."* Growth in our relationship with God results from training in the spiritual disciplines. It happens whenever we become intensely serious about learning from Jesus how to arrange our lives. Spiritual disciplines are the practices we live by that enable us to do what we cannot do by willpower

alone. These practices help us grow in the ability to love God and people—the true indicators of spiritual well-being.

Would you say that you are *training* to become more like Christ, or *trying* to be more like Christ? Why?

John Ortberg emphasizes that we can't transform ourselves; God transforms us. How would you describe the difference between spiritual training and self-transformation? In what way(s) have you attempted self-transformation?

You will have the opportunity to further develop a personal spiritual training plan as this series progresses. For now, write down a few ideas of what spiritual training might involve for you.

PLANNING NOTES

PERSONAL JOURNEY: TO DO ON YOUR OWN

Set aside some time to reflect on the following questions:

1. In *The Life You've Always Wanted,* John Ortberg wrote, "Your story is the story of transformation. You will not always be as you are now; the day is coming when you will be something incomparably better—or worse."

    In which direction are you presently being transformed?

    Is this where you want to go? Why or why not?

2. It is not always easy to know when we are settling for pseudo-transformation rather than real transformation, but the burden of trying to satisfy the demands of a superficial, boundary-marker oriented spirituality will exhaust us. The following questions can help you identify signs of an inauthentic spirituality. This self-assessment is for your eyes only. Be as honest as possible so you can clear the slate and open yourself up to God's transforming work in your life.

    In what way(s) am I preoccupied with *appearing* to be spiritual?

    In which area(s) am I becoming judgmental, exclusive, or proud?

    To what degree am I becoming less approachable to other people?

    In what way(s) am I becoming weary of pursuing spiritual growth?

    In what way(s) do I measure my spiritual life by superficial standards?

    Which "boundary markers" do I use to set myself apart from other people?

    Now pray that God will guide you as you think about your life today and the life you've always wanted. Ask him to speak to your heart and begin transforming you through the remaining sessions of this study.

PERSONAL JOURNEY:
TO DO ON YOUR OWN

Set aside some time to reflect on the following questions:

1. In *The Life You've Always Wanted,* John Ortberg wrote, "Your story is the story of transformation. You will not always be as you are now; the day is coming when you will be something incomparably better—or worse."

   In which direction are you presently being transformed?

   Is this where you want to go? Why or why not?

2. It is not always easy to know when we are settling for pseudo-transformation rather than real transformation, but the burden of trying to satisfy the demands of a superficial, boundary-marker oriented spirituality will exhaust us. The following questions can help you identify signs of an inauthentic spirituality. This self-assessment is for your eyes only. Be as honest as possible so you can clear the slate and open yourself up to God's transforming work in your life.

PLANNING NOTES

In what way(s) am I preoccupied with *appearing* to be spiritual?

In which area(s) am I becoming judgmental, exclusive, or proud?

To what degree am I becoming less approachable to other people?

In what way(s) am I becoming weary of pursuing spiritual growth?

In what way(s) do I measure my spiritual life by superficial standards?

Which "boundary markers" do I use to set myself apart from other people?

Now pray that God will guide you as you think about your life today and the life you've always wanted. Ask him to speak to your heart and begin transforming you through the remaining sessions of this study.

CLOSING MEDITATION

1 MINUTE

Dear God, today we've looked at what spiritual life really is, and what you say about us. Thank you for creating us as masterpieces. Help us to remember that this fallen world is just part of the story, that your kingdom has come and we can live in it today. You offer us the possibility of spiritual transformation, of becoming who you created us to be. Help us to use the opportunities we have to learn from you how to live like Jesus. We need your power for extraordinary change. We long to live in your presence in ways that express your love and joy to people around us. Amen.

Slowing Down
and Celebrating

BEFORE YOU LEAD
Synopsis

This session will focus on two spiritual disciplines that are particularly important in light of the way most of us live. We will explore the discipline of slowing and discover the practice of celebration.

If you're tempted to skip over these spiritual disciplines and get to the "important stuff," it's a sure sign you're afflicted by "hurry sickness"! In fact, most of us have fallen victim to it. We are haunted by the fear that there are not enough hours in the day to do what needs to be done. We buy gadgets that promise to help us save time, then we add more things to our to-do lists. We continually strive to do more and do it faster.

The essential truth we tend to forget is that we simply cannot follow Jesus at a constant sprint. It is impossible to think what Jesus would think, feel what he would feel, perceive what he would perceive, and do what he would do in a hurry. Hurry keeps our focus on the cares and pleasures of life and prevents Jesus' perspective from taking root in our hearts. Hurry keeps us from living and loving well. Hurry is a great enemy of spiritual growth, so we must ruthlessly eliminate it from our lives.

By following the example of Jesus, we can learn to defeat hurry sickness. Although Jesus was always busy, he was never hurried. He regularly took time alone to nurture his life-giving connection with his Father, so his priorities were always ordered according to his Father's will. By practicing the discipline of slowing, we too can learn to become unhurried people. When we build times of solitude into our lives, we remove ourselves from the forces of daily life that otherwise mold us. We withdraw from noise, people, activities, and responsibilities in order to restore our connection with God.

Our connection with God is intended to produce more in us than a well-ordered life, however. It ought to produce joy! It is a sad reality, but for many Christians, joy is highly underrated. Yet it is impossible to truly know God until we understand that he is the happiest being in the universe. Not only that, God longs for us to be filled with his joy.

Joy is so essential that God commands his people to be joyful. Although the church readily overlooks it, joylessness is a serious sin. It causes people to misunderstand God because they attribute to him the grim, judgmental, defensive, and soul-wearying spirit of many who claim to be his followers. So part of this session explores the transforming discipline of celebration and highlights practical ways to learn to cultivate joy.

What a difference this session can make as participants learn to celebrate joy. They'll learn how, moment by moment, to experience and savor the joy each day brings. They'll learn to direct their hearts toward God in gratitude and delight because he is the giver of every good and perfect gift. They'll also be challenged to anticipate the day when there will be no more death, pain, or tears and all of God's people will experience his indescribable joy to the fullest.

Key Points of This Session

1. *We are a people plagued by "hurry sickness," and hurry causes great harm to our spiritual growth.* Hurry is not merely a shortage of time; it is a disease of the soul. It is not just a disordered schedule; it reflects a disordered heart. Hurry lies behind much of the anger and frustration of modern life. It disrupts our life-giving connection with God and prevents us from receiving love from the Father or giving it to his children. If we want to grow spiritually, we must ruthlessly eliminate hurry from our lives.

2. *The discipline of slowing and the practice of solitude are antidotes to hurry sickness.* To eliminate hurry from our lives doesn't mean we won't be busy. Jesus was often busy, but he was never hurried. His priorities were always ordered according to his life-giving connection with his Father. By practicing the discipline of slowing, we too can learn to become unhurried people. When we practice solitude, we remove ourselves from the forces of daily life that otherwise mold us. We withdraw from noise, people, activities, and responsibilities in order to restore our connection with God.

3. *As creatures made in the image of God, we are to reflect his joy in life.* Joy is at the heart of God's plan for us because joy is at the heart of God. We cannot truly know God until we understand that he is the happiest being in the universe. He longs for us to be filled with his joy. It is so important to him that he commands us to be joyful and urges us to participate in celebration, which trains us to experience joy in life.

Suggested Reading

Chapters four and five of *The Life You've Always Wanted*

SESSION OUTLINE

55 MINUTES

I. Introduction (5 minutes)
Welcome
What's to Come
Questions to Think About

II. Video Presentation: "Slowing Down and Celebrating" (13 minutes)

III. Group Discovery (30 minutes)
Video Highlights (5 minutes)
Small Group Exploration (10 minutes)
Large Group Exploration (10 minutes)
Group Discussion (5 minutes)

IV. Personal Journey (6 minutes)

V. Closing Meditation (1 minute)

In the video, John Ortberg uses soap bubbles as a metaphor for joy. You may want to consider doing this for your group. As of this writing, party and discount stores sell soap bubble party favors for less than five dollars for a box of twenty-four. Or, if you want to celebrate in a big way, bubble machines can be purchased for less than fifteen dollars.

As much as we complain about it, we are drawn to hurry. It makes us feel important. It keeps the adrenaline pumping. It means we don't have to look too closely at the heart or life.

—John Ortberg

Slowing Down
and Celebrating

INTRODUCTION

5 MINUTES

Welcome

> Participant's Guide page 29.
>
> Welcome participants to *The Life You've Always Wanted,* session two, "Slowing Down and Celebrating."

What's to Come

We're going to continue our study by considering two essential practices that some of us may never have thought were important spiritual disciplines. In fact, we may be too hurried to notice what we've been missing!

We will explore the discipline of slowing down and the practice of solitude. We will find out why we must ruthlessly eliminate hurry from our lives. We also will turn our eyes to the joy that explodes from the heart of God in everything he does. We'll find out ways to practice the discipline of celebration so that we can cultivate this gift and experience God's joy in everyday life.

Let's begin by considering a few questions related to how we live and enjoy our lives. These questions are on page 30 of your Participant's Guide.

Slowing Down and Celebrating

SESSION TWO

As much as we complain about it, we are drawn to hurry. It makes us feel important. It keeps the adrenaline pumping. It means we don't have to look too closely at the heart or life.

—John Ortberg

29

QUESTIONS TO THINK ABOUT

1. How many times a day do you estimate you think to yourself, *Oh, I'd better hurry and . . . ?* What are some of the reasons you feel you have to "hurry" through life?

2. If someone were to say, "I think you would benefit from a day of solitude," how would you respond? What do you think such a day would be like?

3. What is the most joyful event you have ever witnessed or in which you have ever participated? What made it meaningful to you?

PLANNING NOTES

Questions to Think About

Participant's Guide page 30.

As time permits, ask participants to respond to two or more of the following questions.

1. How many times a day do you estimate you think to yourself, *Oh, I'd better hurry and . . . ?* What are some of the reasons you feel you have to "hurry" through life?

    When we stop to consider it, most of us think this phrase (or a similar one that indicates the same problem) at least half a dozen times a day—maybe as often as twenty-five or more times a day! Make sure participants realize how predominant the need to hurry is in their lives—it's easy to overlook. We hurry because we get caught up in the tyranny of the urgent, other people expect us to do something or be somewhere, we think that hurrying will buy us more time, we feel more important if we have a lot to do, we hurry to get things done so we can have more time for ourselves, etc.

2. If someone were to say, "I think you would benefit from a day of solitude," how would you respond? What do you think such a day would be like?

    Answers will vary, but don't expect many participants to respond with enthusiasm. Some may welcome it, but quickly add, "It will never happen in my life!" Some may say, "You've got to be kidding!" Still others may say, "What for? What would I do?" Encourage participants to actually describe what they think a day of solitude would be like. Many may not have thought in this way before. Some may describe such a day in terms of quietness, peace, or relief from demanding responsibilities. Others may imagine it as being alone or bored, lacking stimulation, unable to accomplish anything, etc.

QUESTIONS TO THINK ABOUT

1. How many times a day do you estimate you think to yourself, *Oh, I'd better hurry and . . . ?* What are some of the reasons you feel you have to "hurry" through life?

2. If someone were to say, "I think you would benefit from a day of solitude," how would you respond? What do you think such a day would be like?

3. What is the most joyful event you have ever witnessed or in which you have ever participated? What made it meaningful to you?

PLANNING NOTES

3. What is the most joyful event you have ever witnessed or in which you have ever participated? What made it meaningful to you?

    Some participants will have an immediate answer while others may need to think about this one for a minute. Expect varied responses—weddings, homecomings, births, parties, festivals, accomplishments. However, joy may be found in brief, quiet, or private moments as well—for example, the first time a couple hears their baby's heartbeat or a sincere expression of praise or admiration. Joy may also be expressed following a rainstorm during a drought or when a person first sees breakers at the seashore. The objective is to help participants begin looking for and thinking about moments of joy in their world and the impact joy can have on daily life.

    Let's keep these ideas in mind as we view the video. There is space to take notes on page 31 of your Participant's Guide.

VIDEO PRESENTATION: "SLOWING DOWN AND CELEBRATING"

13 MINUTES

> Participant's Guide page 31.

Video Observations

"Hurry sickness"

The discipline of slowing

"Dee dah day" moments

The connection between God and joy

QUESTIONS TO THINK ABOUT

1. How many times a day do you estimate you think to yourself, *Oh, I'd better hurry and . . . ?* What are some of the reasons you feel you have to "hurry" through life?

2. If someone were to say, "I think you would benefit from a day of solitude," how would you respond? What do you think such a day would be like?

3. What is the most joyful event you have ever witnessed or in which you have ever participated? What made it meaningful to you?

VIDEO OBSERVATIONS

"Hurry sickness"

The discipline of slowing

"Dee dah day" moments

The connection between God and joy

PLANNING NOTES

GROUP DISCOVERY

30 MINUTES

> **If your group has seven or more members,** use the Video Highlights with the entire group (5 minutes), then break into small groups of three to five people for the Small Group Exploration (10 minutes). Next bring everyone together to complete the Large Group Exploration (10 minutes) and the closing Group Discussion (5 minutes).
>
> **If your group has fewer than seven members,** begin with the Video Highlights (5 minutes), then complete both the Small Group Exploration (10 minutes) and the Large Group Exploration (10 minutes). Wrap up your discovery time with the Group Discussion (5 minutes).

Please turn to page 32 of your Participant's Guide.

Video Highlights • 5 minutes

> Participant's Guide page 32.
>
> As time permits, ask one or more of the following questions, which directly relate to the video the participants have just seen.

1. Why is "hurry sickness" so harmful to our spiritual growth?

   SUGGESTED RESPONSE: *Hurry prevents us from listening to God and loving others well. Hurry takes a physical, mental, and emotional toll. We can become so trapped in "hurry mode" that we don't spend time alone with God to focus on him and connect with what he wants to reveal to us. When we're in a hurry, we don't stop long enough to consider how Jesus would think or what he would do if he were in our place.*

2. Many of us tend to avoid solitude. Which characteristics of solitude offend us? Which of our attitudes cause us to resist solitude?

   Why?

   SUGGESTED RESPONSE: *When we're busy and consumed with hurry it seems impossible to get away for times of solitude. Many of us are so used to busyness that we feel uncomfortable alone. We*

   and quiet.

VIDEO HIGHLIGHTS

1. Why is "hurry sickness" so harmful to our spiritual growth?

Oh for the Joy of It!

Early in the Israelites' history, God (speaking through Moses) established times of celebration. During these times, God's people would do things that filled them with joy, and they would identify those things as blessings from God. Some of the feasts included:

The Feast of Weeks celebrating the dedication of the firstfruits of the wheat harvest, the last crop to ripen (Leviticus 23:15–21).

The Feast of Passover that combined Passover, which celebrated the angel of death passing over the Hebrew households in Egypt (Leviticus 23:5), and the Feast of Unleavened Bread, which commemorated the first seven days of the Exodus (Leviticus 23:6–8).

The Feast of Tabernacles, which commemorated the Israelites' wandering in the desert (Leviticus 23:33–36).

Here's a thought to ponder: How might Christians today live differently if we designated certain days to specifically celebrate God's goodness — to celebrate a bountiful harvest, to celebrate employment, to celebrate the unique beauty of where we live, to truly celebrate redemption as a gift from God?

---

2. Many of us tend to avoid solitude. Which characteristics of solitude offend us? Which of our attitudes cause us to resist solitude?

3. What did you think when John Ortberg spoke of God as being deeply joyful? Why do you think God commands, rather than suggests, that we be joyful?

4. In the Old Testament, God commanded the Israelites to celebrate on many occasions. From a spiritual perspective, what is the point of celebration?

PLANNING NOTES

Condition ourselves to hurry — don't even realize it.

Christians —

Oh for the Joy of It!

Early in the Israelites' history, God (speaking through Moses) established times of celebration. During these times, God's people would do things that filled them with joy, and they would identify those things as blessings from God. Some of the feasts included:

The Feast of Weeks celebrating the dedication of the firstfruits of the wheat harvest, the last crop to ripen (Leviticus 23:15–21).

The Feast of Passover that combined Passover, which celebrated the angel of death passing over the Hebrew households in Egypt (Leviticus 23:5), and the Feast of Unleavened Bread, which commemorated the first seven days of the Exodus (Leviticus 23:6–8).

The Feast of Tabernacles, which commemorated the Israelites' wandering in the desert (Leviticus 23:33–36).

Purim — Esther

Here's a thought to ponder: How might Christians today live differently if we designated certain days to specifically celebrate God's goodness — to celebrate a bountiful harvest, to celebrate employment, to celebrate the unique beauty of where we live, to truly celebrate redemption as a gift from God?

We don't want to look at our lives introspectively.

think we should be doing something to prove our worth and value. We're afraid of being alone, of not having other people around us. Solitude may threaten our identity because we do not know who we are apart from what we have done and are doing. We are unfamiliar with the benefits of solitude.

3. What did you think when John Ortberg spoke of God as being deeply joyful? Why do you think God commands, rather than suggests, that we be joyful?

    SUGGESTED RESPONSE: *These will vary. This may be a new concept for some participants. When people list the attributes of God, joy usually isn't in the top three! The fact that he commands us to be joyful indicates his commitment to joy. He wants us to delight in him and his goodness and to reflect his joy to other people around us. If we don't reflect his joy, we misrepresent his character—we're guilty of false advertising!*

4. In the Old Testament, God commanded the Israelites to celebrate on many occasions. From a spiritual perspective, what is the point of celebration?

VIDEO HIGHLIGHTS

1. Why is "hurry sickness" so harmful to our spiritual growth?

Oh for the Joy of It!

Early in the Israelites' history, God (speaking through Moses) established times of celebration. During these times, God's people would do things that filled them with joy, and they would identify those things as blessings from God. Some of the feasts included:

The Feast of Weeks celebrating the dedication of the firstfruits of the wheat harvest, the last crop to ripen (Leviticus 23:15–21).

The Feast of Passover that combined Passover, which celebrated the angel of death passing over the Hebrew households in Egypt (Leviticus 23:5), and the Feast of Unleavened Bread, which commemorated the first seven days of the Exodus (Leviticus 23:6–8).

The Feast of Tabernacles, which commemorated the Israelites' wandering in the desert (Leviticus 23:33–36).

Here's a thought to ponder: How might Christians today live differently if we designated certain days to specifically celebrate God's goodness — to celebrate a bountiful harvest, to celebrate employment, to celebrate the unique beauty of where we live, to truly celebrate redemption as a gift from God?

---

2. Many of us tend to avoid solitude. Which characteristics of solitude offend us? Which of our attitudes cause us to resist solitude?

3. What did you think when John Ortberg spoke of God as being deeply joyful? Why do you think God commands, rather than suggests, that we be joyful?

4. In the Old Testament, God commanded the Israelites to celebrate on many occasions. From a spiritual perspective, what is the point of celebration?

PLANNING NOTES

*Christmas
Easter*

SUGGESTED RESPONSE: *The Israelites experienced many hardships and, like us, needed to set aside time to remember and enjoy the goodness of God. God knew the value of having them do things that filled them with joy and reminded them that he was the giver of every good and perfect gift. Celebration draws us closer to God as we see and feel what he has given us. Celebration trains us for joy. It teaches us to find delight where we wouldn't have noticed it before.*

We will continue our exploration by taking a hard look at hurry sickness and its impact on our spiritual growth. Please break into small groups of three to five and complete the Small Group Exploration that begins on page 34 of your Participant's Guide. I will give you a one-minute notice before we rejoin for our Large Group Exploration and Discussion.

Small Group Exploration • 10 minutes

> Participant's Guide page 34.

Confronting Our Hurry Sickness

Hovercraft

It's no secret that most of us lead hurried, harried lives. John Ortberg describes the American lifestyle as being so rushed and preoccupied that we don't actually live life, we just skim over it! Yet racing through life at breakneck speed isn't healthy physically or spiritually.

Hurry sickness is more than a disordered schedule; it reflects a disordered heart. Hurry disrupts our life-giving connection with God, so if we want to grow spiritually we must train ourselves to eliminate hurry. We have no greater example of this than the life of Jesus. Let's see how Jesus faced his busy life and consider what we can change to eliminate hurry in our lives.

1. Read Mark 6:30–46, which is an account of a day in the life of Jesus.

   a. What kind of day did Jesus have?

      SUGGESTED RESPONSE: *It was a very busy day! He had so much interaction with people that he and his disciples had no time to eat, so they traveled by boat to a solitary place. But eager crowds of people raced to meet him there, so Jesus ended up teaching until late in the day. Then he served dinner for more*

2. Many of us tend to avoid solitude. Which characteristics of solitude offend us? Which of our attitudes cause us to resist solitude?

3. What did you think when John Ortberg spoke of God as being deeply joyful? Why do you think God commands, rather than suggests, that we be joyful?

4. In the Old Testament, God commanded the Israelites to celebrate on many occasions. From a spiritual perspective, what is the point of celebration?

34 • The Life You've Always Wanted Participant's Guide

SMALL GROUP EXPLORATION

Confronting Our Hurry Sickness

It's no secret that most of us lead hurried, harried lives. John Ortberg describes the American lifestyle as being so rushed and preoccupied that we don't actually live life, we just skim over it! Yet racing through life at breakneck speed isn't healthy physically or spiritually.

Hurry sickness is more than a disordered schedule; it reflects a disordered heart. Hurry disrupts our life-giving connection with God, so if we want to grow spiritually we must train ourselves to eliminate hurry. We have no greater example of this than the life of Jesus. Let's see how Jesus faced his busy life and consider what we can change to eliminate hurry in our lives.

1. Read Mark 6:30–46, which is an account of a day in the life of Jesus.

   a. What kind of day did Jesus have?

   b. How do you think you might have handled that day if you had been in Jesus' shoes?

PLANNING NOTES

than five thousand people. Afterward, he sent his disciples on ahead, sent the crowd home, and went off by himself to pray.

b. How do you think you might have handled that day if you had been in Jesus' shoes?

SUGGESTED RESPONSE: *That day would have been a handful for anyone! Ask participants to indicate when they would have gone into overload.*

c. What is significant about what Jesus did at the end of this busy day? (See Luke 5:15–16 also.)

SUGGESTED RESPONSE: *Although he was surrounded by people who wanted his attention, Jesus withdrew from everyone else in order to be alone and pray. He would not neglect his need for solitude and communion with his Father. He was busy, but never too hurried to keep his priorities straight.*

2. Two friends of Jesus (the sisters Mary and Martha) shed some light on the impact of hurry sickness on our lives. Read Luke 10:38–42 and note what is happening spiritually and relationally. Note also how Jesus viewed this situation.

SUGGESTED RESPONSE: *Whereas Mary set aside everything to be with Jesus and to hear what he said, Martha was "hurried." Martha was distracted by all the preparations involved in Jesus' stay. She not only was missing out on her spiritual relationship with Jesus, her focus on what had to be done disrupted her relationship with her sister. Jesus gently rebuked Martha and encouraged her to focus on the one important thing.*

Hurried people get irritated with those who live at a slower pace.

3. When John Ortberg says we must "ruthlessly eliminate hurry," he doesn't mean we just cross things off our to-do list. We eliminate hurry by setting the priorities of our heart in order. The Bible frequently cautions us against being consumed (or disordered) by the priorities of this world—accumulation of wealth, concern about food and shelter, desire for recognition or power—all of which drive us to be hurried people. The following Scripture passages provide perspective and instruction on how to "order" our hearts. What do they reveal is beneficial or harmful to us?

a. Matthew 16:26

SMALL GROUP EXPLORATION

Confronting Our Hurry Sickness

It's no secret that most of us lead hurried, harried lives. John Ortberg describes the American lifestyle as being so rushed and preoccupied that we don't actually live life, we just skim over it! Yet racing through life at breakneck speed isn't healthy physically or spiritually.

Hurry sickness is more than a disordered schedule; it reflects a disordered heart. Hurry disrupts our life-giving connection with God, so if we want to grow spiritually we must train ourselves to eliminate hurry. We have no greater example of this than the life of Jesus. Let's see how Jesus faced his busy life and consider what we can change to eliminate hurry in our lives.

1. Read Mark 6:30–46, which is an account of a day in the life of Jesus.

   a. What kind of day did Jesus have?

   b. How do you think you might have handled that day if you had been in Jesus' shoes?

   c. What is significant about what Jesus did at the end of this busy day? (See Luke 5:15–16 also.)

2. Two friends of Jesus (the sisters Mary and Martha) shed some light on the impact of hurry sickness on our lives. Read Luke 10:38–42 and note what is happening spiritually and relationally. Note also how Jesus viewed this situation.

3. When John Ortberg says we must "ruthlessly eliminate hurry," he doesn't mean we just cross things off our to-do list. We eliminate hurry by setting the priorities of our heart in order. The Bible frequently cautions us against being consumed (or disordered) by the priorities of this world—accumulation of wealth, concern about food and shelter, desire for recognition or power—all of which drive us to be hurried people. The following Scripture passages provide perspective and instruction on how to "order" our hearts. What do they reveal is beneficial or harmful to us?

   a. Matthew 16:26

PLANNING NOTES

SUGGESTED RESPONSE: *We are free to pursue all the world has to offer, but there is a terrible price to pay. What have we really gained if we lose our souls in the process?*

b. 1 Timothy 6:6–7

SUGGESTED RESPONSE: *What good is it to gain "stuff"? We have nothing when we are born and take nothing with us when we die. The real gain is godliness with contentment. (Note that contentment could be justifiably defined as an opposite of hurry sickness.)*

c. Philippians 3:18–21

SUGGESTED RESPONSE: *These strong words emphasize that focusing on earthly things is actually destructive. In contrast, when we view ourselves as citizens of heaven (and this would be an intentional focus on God's kingdom), we are transformed by Christ's power. This means we are growing spiritually—becoming like him.*

4. If we don't want hurry to rule our lives, we need to take steps to slow down. John Ortberg calls these steps the discipline of slowing down and the practice of solitude.

a. When we feel hurried, when we are pressured and pressed from every angle, what does the Bible tell us to do? What is the result? (See 1 Peter 5:7 and Philippians 4:6, respectively.)

SUGGESTED RESPONSE: *We are to give all our anxieties to God, who cares for us. We are not to be anxious about anything but to present our requests, with thanksgiving, to God. We can slow down and rest in Christ's loving care for us.*

b. In addition to quieting our spirit by giving our cares to God and trusting him to enable us to accomplish all we need to get done, we can deliberately choose ways not to hurry. We can, for example, place ourselves in positions where we have to wait or do things more slowly, such as driving in the slow lane. What is a good way for you to practice deliberate slowing?

SUGGESTED RESPONSE: *Participants should write down at least one step they can take to slow down.*

(handwritten margin notes:)

Actually drive the speed limit?

Intentionally choose longer check out line so you have time to pray!

Arrive early for an appointment and use time to read or pray.

c. What is significant about what Jesus did at the end of this busy day? (See Luke 5:15–16 also.)

2. Two friends of Jesus (the sisters Mary and Martha) shed some light on the impact of hurry sickness on our lives. Read Luke 10:38–42 and note what is happening spiritually and relationally. Note also how Jesus viewed this situation.

3. When John Ortberg says we must "ruthlessly eliminate hurry," he doesn't mean we just cross things off our to-do list. We eliminate hurry by setting the priorities of our heart in order. The Bible frequently cautions us against being consumed (or disordered) by the priorities of this world—accumulation of wealth, concern about food and shelter, desire for recognition or power—all of which drive us to be hurried people. The following Scripture passages provide perspective and instruction on how to "order" our hearts. What do they reveal is beneficial or harmful to us?

a. Matthew 16:26

PLANNING NOTES

_____

_____

_____

_____

_____

_____

_____

_____

b. 1 Timothy 6:6–7

c. Philippians 3:18–21

4. If we don't want hurry to rule our lives, we need to take steps to slow down. John Ortberg calls these steps the discipline of slowing down and the practice of solitude.

a. When we feel hurried, when we are pressured and pressed from every angle, what does the Bible tell us to do? What is the result? (See 1 Peter 5:7 and Philippians 4:6, respectively.)

b. In addition to quieting our spirit by giving our cares to God and trusting him to enable us to accomplish all we need to get done, we can deliberately choose ways not

to hurry. We can, for example, place ourselves in positions where we have to wait or do things more slowly, such as driving in the slow lane. What is a good way for you to practice deliberate slowing?

c. Every day, responsibilities pull us in many directions, so we each need times of solitude—times to withdraw, take a deep breath, focus on God, recharge, and evaluate. When can you find (or carve out) a daily moment for solitude? Identify at least two possibilities for regular, longer times of solitude.

c. Every day, responsibilities pull us in many directions, so we each need times of solitude—times to withdraw, take a deep breath, focus on God, recharge, and evaluate. When can you find (or carve out) a daily moment for solitude? Identify at least two possibilities for regular, longer times of solitude.

SUGGESTED RESPONSE: *Participants should identify their daily moment for solitude. It may be as simple as getting to work a few minutes early for some quiet moments, spending a short time alone in the car while waiting to pick up children, taking ten uninterrupted minutes alone before going to bed. The longer periods of solitude may be a few hours a week, or a day away every month or six weeks—but remember, no agenda!*

Let participants know when one minute remains.

When time is up, ask the groups to rejoin as one group.

Large Group Exploration • 10 minutes

Participant's Guide page 38.

God Wants Us to Mirror His Joy

G. K. Chesterton wrote about children having such "abounding vitality" that they want to do, see, or hear the same things again and again and again. Although the monotony of repetition nearly kills grown-ups, it thrills children. And Chesterton thinks it is possible that, like a child, God exults in monotony. He writes in *Orthodoxy:*

It is possible that God says every morning, "Do it again" to the sun; and every evening, "Do it again" to the moon. It may not be automatic necessity that makes all daisies alike; it may be that God makes every daisy separately, but has never got tired of making them. It may be that He has the eternal appetite of infancy; *for we have sinned and grown old, and our Father is younger than we.*

In other words, many of us live as the joy-impaired children of a joy-infused God! So let's see what God has to say about joy and how he wants it to influence our lives.

to hurry. We can, for example, place ourselves in positions where we have to wait or do things more slowly, such as driving in the slow lane. What is a good way for you to practice deliberate slowing?

c. Every day, responsibilities pull us in many directions, so we each need times of solitude—times to withdraw, take a deep breath, focus on God, recharge, and evaluate. When can you find (or carve out) a daily moment for solitude? Identify at least two possibilities for regular, longer times of solitude.

---

38 • The Life You've Always Wanted Participant's Guide

LARGE GROUP EXPLORATION

God Wants Us to Mirror His Joy

G. K. Chesterton wrote about children having such "abounding vitality" that they want to do, see, or hear the same things again and again and again. Although the monotony of repetition nearly kills grown-ups, it thrills children. And Chesterton thinks it is possible that, like a child, God exults in monotony. He writes in *Orthodoxy*:

> It is possible that God says every morning, "Do it again" to the sun; and every evening, "Do it again" to the moon. It may not be automatic necessity that makes all daisies alike; it may be that God makes every daisy separately, but has never got tired of making them. It may be that He has the eternal appetite of infancy; *for we have sinned and grown old, and our Father is younger than we.*

In other words, many of us live as the joy-impaired children of a joy-infused God! So let's see what God has to say about joy and how he wants it to influence our lives.

1. In Genesis 1, we read a day-by-day account of God's creation of the universe.

   a. What pattern is repeated throughout the process of creation, and what does it reveal about God? (See Genesis 1:3–5, 9–12, 14–18, 20–21, 24–25, 31.)

PLANNING NOTES

[handwritten note in left margin: Plan / Act / Enjoy / Children can do crafts]

1. In Genesis 1, we read a day-by-day account of God's creation of the universe.

   a. What pattern is repeated throughout the process of creation, and what does it reveal about God? (See Genesis 1:3–5, 9–12, 14–18, 20–21, 24–25, and 31.)

      SUGGESTED RESPONSE: *Over and over again we read, "God said … And it was so," and "God saw that it was good." God was delighted with his creation. He delighted in making it— creating more each day. When it was all done, he looked it over and it "was very good," which certainly would have brought joy to his heart.*

   b. What other indications of God's pleasure and joy do we see in Genesis 1? (Note especially verses 22, 27–28.)

      SUGGESTED RESPONSE: *God obviously was excited about what he was creating. In verses 14–21, there is a sense that God "was on a roll," excited, delighted, and inspired by each new element of his handiwork. We can almost feel the overflowing nature of his joy when he blessed his creation and commanded it to be fruitful. It was so good, God wanted to see more and more of it!*

2. In *The Life You've Always Wanted*, John Ortberg describes Jesus as the "Joy-bringer." What did Jesus bring, and what does it have to do with joy? (See Matthew 4:23; 1 Peter 1:8–9.)

   SUGGESTED RESPONSE: *Jesus brought the good news of the gospel, which fills those who believe with joy because they are receiving salvation for their souls. Salvation is certainly a cause for joy!*

3. Toward the end of his life on earth, Jesus prepared himself and his followers for his departure. What was his specific desire and concern for his followers? (See John 15:9–11; 17:1, 13.)

   SUGGESTED RESPONSE: *Jesus wanted his followers to be filled with his joy. He instructed them how to have the same joy he had— to obey God and to remain in God's love. He prayed that their joy would be full—complete, in full measure.*

LARGE GROUP EXPLORATION

God Wants Us to Mirror His Joy

C. K. Chesterton wrote about children having such "abounding vitality" that they want to do, see, or hear the same things again and again and again. Although the monotony of repetition nearly kills grown-ups, it thrills children. And Chesterton thinks it is possible that, like a child, God exults in monotony. He writes in *Orthodoxy:*

> It is possible that God says every morning, "Do it again" to the sun; and every evening, "Do it again" to the moon. It may not be automatic necessity that makes all daisies alike; it may be that God makes every daisy separately, but has never got tired of making them. It may be that He has the eternal appetite of infancy; *for we have sinned and grown old, and our Father is younger than we.*

In other words, many of us live as the joy-impaired children of a joy-infused God! So let's see what God has to say about joy and how he wants it to influence our lives.

1. In Genesis 1, we read a day-by-day account of God's creation of the universe.

   a. What pattern is repeated throughout the process of creation, and what does it reveal about God? (See Genesis 1:3–5, 9–12, 14–18, 20–21, 24–25, 31.)

   b. What other indications of God's pleasure and joy do we see in Genesis 1? (Note especially verses 22, 27–28.)

2. In *The Life You've Always Wanted*, John Ortberg describes Jesus as the "Joy-bringer." What did Jesus bring, and what does it have to do with joy? (See Matthew 4:23; 1 Peter 1:8–9.)

3. Toward the end of his life on earth, Jesus prepared himself and his followers for his departure. What was his specific desire and concern for his followers? (See John 15:9–11; 17:1, 13.)

4. When are we to express joy and why is it so important? (See Philippians 4:4; 1 Thessalonians 5:16–18.)

PLANNING NOTES

4. When are we to express joy and why is it so important? (See Philippians 4:4; 1 Thessalonians 5:16–18.)

SUGGESTED RESPONSE: *The apostle Paul told the Philippians to "rejoice in the Lord always" and repeated it for emphasis. He used even stronger terms in his letter to the Thessalonians, where he wrote that expressing joy—just like prayer and thanksgiving—is God's will for us. So joy is a command, not an option.*

5. When the exiles returned to Israel, they focused on obeying God's law. As they began to understand God's law, they grieved over their sinfulness, but God commanded them to celebrate what he had done. What did the people do, and what was the result? (See Nehemiah 8:9–12, 17.)

SUGGESTED RESPONSE: *Nehemiah and the Levites instructed the people to stop grieving and to celebrate because the "joy of the Lord" was their strength. So they turned from their grieving and celebrated with great joy. Their celebration was so great there had been nothing like it for generations.*

6. What can God's people look forward to in eternity? (See Isaiah 35:9–10.)

SUGGESTED RESPONSE: *It will be a place of overwhelming and everlasting joy.*

Group Discussion • 5 minutes

Participant's Guide page 41.

As time permits, discuss the following questions that will help participants explore their understanding of the concepts covered in this session.

NOTE: If you have chosen to use soap bubbles during this session, now is the time. You may share them at any time during this discussion—the point is to add delight and emphasize the importance of celebration.

Now it's time for us to wrap up our discovery time. Please turn to page 41, and let's talk together about the impact of hurry and a lack of joy on daily life.

b. What other indications of God's pleasure and joy do we see in Genesis 1? (Note especially verses 22, 27–28.)

2. In *The Life You've Always Wanted*, John Ortberg describes Jesus as the "Joy-bringer." What did Jesus bring, and what does it have to do with joy? (See Matthew 4:23; 1 Peter 1:8–9.)

3. Toward the end of his life on earth, Jesus prepared himself and his followers for his departure. What was his specific desire and concern for his followers? (See John 15:9–11; 17:1, 13.)

4. When are we to express joy and why is it so important? (See Philippians 4:4; 1 Thessalonians 5:16–18.)

PLANNING NOTES

_____

_____

_____

_____

_____

_____

_____

_____

_____

5. When the exiles returned to Israel, they focused on obeying God's law. As they began to understand God's law, they grieved over their sinfulness, but God commanded them to celebrate what he had done. What did the people do, and what was the result? (See Nehemiah 8:9–12, 17.)

6. What can God's people look forward to in eternity? (See Isaiah 35:9–10.)

GROUP DISCUSSION

1. What is the real difference between being *busy* and being *hurried?*

2. What did you learn about joy today? In what ways might understanding more about the joy of the Lord affect your view of joy?

3. As you look at daily life, can you identify any "dee dah day" moments you've been overlooking, or that many of us overlook? How might life change if we left room in our hearts to enjoy these "dee dah day" moments?

4. In light of what we have studied during this session, which aspects of spiritual life do you think ought to prompt a "dee dah day" response? How often do you respond to these with joy? How often do you see others respond to these with joy? Why do you think we sometimes lack joy?

1. What is the real difference between being *busy* and being *hurried?*

2. What did you learn about joy today? In what ways might understanding more about the joy of the Lord affect your view of joy?

3. As you look at daily life, can you identify any "dee dah day" moments you've been overlooking, or that many of us overlook? How might life change if we left room in our hearts to enjoy these "dee dah day" moments?

4. In light of what we have studied during this session, which aspects of spiritual life do you think ought to prompt a "dee dah day" response? How often do you respond to these with joy? How often do you see others respond to these with joy? Why do you think we sometimes lack joy?

PERSONAL JOURNEY: TO DO NOW

6 MINUTES

> Participant's Guide page 42.

Now let's turn to page 42 and spend a few minutes alone with God to review the key points and begin considering how what we've explored today can make a difference in our daily lives.

1. *We are a people plagued by "hurry sickness," and hurry causes great harm to our spiritual growth.* Hurry is not merely a shortage of time; it is a disease of the soul. It is not just a disordered schedule; it reflects a disordered heart. Hurry lies behind much of the anger and frustration of modern life. It disrupts our life-giving connection with God and prevents us from receiving love from the Father or giving it to his children. If we want to grow spiritually, we must ruthlessly eliminate hurry from our lives.

   In what ways has hurry sickness hurt you, people around you, and your relationship with God?

GROUP DISCUSSION

1. What is the real difference between being *busy* and being *hurried?*

2. What did you learn about joy today? In what ways might understanding more about the joy of the Lord affect your view of joy?

3. As you look at daily life, can you identify any "dee dah day" moments you've been overlooking, or that many of us overlook? How might life change if we left room in our hearts to enjoy these "dee dah day" moments?

4. In light of what we have studied during this session, which aspects of spiritual life do you think ought to prompt a "dee dah day" response? How often do you respond to these with joy? How often do you see others respond to these with joy? Why do you think we sometimes lack joy?

---

42 • The Life You've Always Wanted Participant's Guide

PERSONAL JOURNEY: TO DO NOW

1. *We are a people plagued by "hurry sickness," and hurry causes great harm to our spiritual growth.* Hurry is not merely a shortage of time; it is a disease of the soul. It is not just a disordered schedule; it reflects a disordered heart. Hurry lies behind much of the anger and frustration of modern life. It disrupts our life-giving connection with God and prevents us from receiving love from the Father or giving it to his children. If we want to grow spiritually, we must ruthlessly eliminate hurry from our lives.

   In what ways has hurry sickness hurt you, people around you, and your relationship with God?

2. *The discipline of slowing and the practice of solitude are antidotes to hurry sickness.* To eliminate hurry from our lives doesn't mean we won't be busy. Jesus was often busy, but he was never hurried. His priorities were always ordered according to his life-giving connection with his Father. By practicing the discipline of slowing, we too can learn to become unhurried people. When we practice solitude, we remove ourselves from the forces of daily life that otherwise mold us. We withdraw from noise, people, activities, and responsibilities in order to restore our connection with God.

   Consider how different your life would be if you approached it from an unhurried perspective, if you ordered your

PLANNING NOTES

2. *The discipline of slowing and the practice of solitude are antidotes to hurry sickness.* To eliminate hurry from our lives doesn't mean we won't be busy. Jesus was often busy, but he was never hurried. His priorities were always ordered according to his life-giving connection with his Father. By practicing the discipline of slowing, we too can learn to become unhurried people. When we practice solitude, we remove ourselves from the forces of daily life that otherwise mold us. We withdraw from noise, people, activities, and responsibilities in order to restore our connection with God.

    Consider how different your life would be if you approached it from an unhurried perspective, if you ordered your priorities according to your relationship with God. Write down specific things you can think or do to eliminate hurry.

3. *As creatures made in the image of God, we are to reflect God's joy in life.* Joy is at the heart of God's plan for us because joy is

Symptoms of hurry sickness	Our perspective when we are hurried	My "unhurried" alternative
Constantly speeding up daily activities	There aren't enough hours in the day so we try to do things faster and become impatient when we have to wait.	
Multi-tasking	We do or think about more than one thing at a time, packing as much into our day as possible.	
Clutter	Things aren't simple. Stuff accumulates. We get weighed down by things we failed to refuse to do.	
Superficiality	We trade wisdom for information and exchange depth for breadth.	
Sunset fatigue	By day's end, we are too tired, drained, or preoccupied to receive love from the Father or give it to people around us.	

42 • The Life You've Always Wanted Participant's Guide

PERSONAL JOURNEY: TO DO NOW

1. *We are a people plagued by "hurry sickness," and hurry causes great harm to our spiritual growth.* Hurry is not merely a shortage of time; it is a disease of the soul. It is not just a disordered schedule; it reflects a disordered heart. Hurry lies behind much of the anger and frustration of modern life. It disrupts our life-giving connection with God and prevents us from receiving love from the Father or giving it to his children. If we want to grow spiritually, we must ruthlessly eliminate hurry from our lives.

   In what ways has hurry sickness hurt you, people around you, and your relationship with God?

2. *The discipline of slowing and the practice of solitude are antidotes to hurry sickness.* To eliminate hurry from our lives doesn't mean we won't be busy. Jesus was often busy, but he was never hurried. His priorities were always ordered according to his life-giving connection with his Father. By practicing the discipline of slowing, we too can learn to become unhurried people. When we practice solitude, we remove ourselves from the forces of daily life that otherwise mold us. We withdraw from noise, people, activities, and responsibilities in order to restore our connection with God.

   Consider how different your life would be if you approached it from an unhurried perspective, if you ordered your

Session Two: Slowing Down and Celebrating • 43

priorities according to your relationship with God. Write down specific things you can think or do to eliminate hurry.

Symptoms of hurry sickness	Our perspective when we are hurried	My "unhurried" alternative
Constantly speeding up daily activities	There aren't enough hours in the day so we try to do things faster and become impatient when we have to wait.	
Multi-tasking	We do or think about more than one thing at a time, packing as much into our day as possible.	
Clutter	Things aren't simple. Stuff accumulates. We get weighed down by things we failed to refuse to do.	
Clutter	We trade wisdom for information and exchange depth for breadth.	
Sunset fatigue	By day's end, we are too tired, drained, or preoccupied to receive love from the Father or give it to people around us.	

3. *As creatures made in the image of God, we are to reflect God's joy in life.* Joy is at the heart of God's plan for us because joy is at the heart of God. We cannot truly know God until we understand that he is the happiest being in the universe. He longs for us to be filled with his joy. It is so important to him that he commands us to be joyful and urges us to participate in celebration, which trains us to experience joy in life.

PLANNING NOTES

at the heart of God. We cannot truly know God until we understand that he is the happiest being in the universe. He longs for us to be filled with his joy. It is so important to him that he commands us to be joyful and urges us to participate in celebration, which trains us to experience joy in life.

Would people close to you describe you as a joyful person? If not, how would they describe you? In what ways would you like their perception to change?

Think over the last day and week and write down "dee dah day" moments that occurred around you.

What was your response to those moments?

What did you benefit from or miss out on related to those moments?

Let participants know when there is one minute remaining.

When time is up, remind participants that they may want to continue their journey on their own time by completing the exercises on pages 45–47 of their Participant's Guide. Then end the session with the Closing Meditation.

priorities according to your relationship with God. Write down specific things you can think or do to eliminate hurry.

Symptoms of hurry sickness	Our perspective when we are hurried	My "unhurried" alternative
Constantly speeding up daily activities	There aren't enough hours in the day so we try to do things faster and become impatient when we have to wait.	
Multi-tasking	We do or think about more than one thing at a time, packing as much into our day as possible.	
Clutter	Things aren't simple. Stuff accumulates. We get weighed down by things we failed to refuse to do.	
Clutter	We trade wisdom for information and exchange depth for breadth.	
Sunset fatigue	By day's end, we are too tired, drained, or preoccupied to receive love from the Father or give it to people around us.	

3. *As creatures made in the image of God, we are to reflect God's joy in life.* Joy is at the heart of God's plan for us because joy is at the heart of God. We cannot truly know God until we understand that he is the happiest being in the universe. He longs for us to be filled with his joy. It is so important to him that he commands us to be joyful and urges us to participate in celebration, which trains us to experience joy in life.

PLANNING NOTES

_____

_____

_____

_____

_____

_____

_____

_____

Would people close to you describe you as a joyful person? If not, how would they describe you? In what ways would you like their perception to change?

Think over the last day and week and write down "dee dah day" moments that occurred around you.

What was your response to those moments?

What did you benefit from or miss out on related to those moments?

PERSONAL JOURNEY: TO DO ON YOUR OWN

Knowledge is not what makes us unhurried or joyful people. We have to train—practice being who we want to become. Set aside some time to practice the disciplines of slowing down and celebration.

The Practice of Daily Solitude: Reviewing the Day with God

It can be difficult to carve out times of extended solitude, but every day you can practice solitude a few minutes at a time. Here's how:

1. Be still for a moment and quiet your mind.
2. Acknowledge that Jesus is present. Invite him to teach you.
3. Go back in your mind to when you first woke up and watch that scene, as if on video. This may lead you to pray for patience, greater love, courage, forgiveness, or other virtues.
4. Continue to reflect on the day, going from scene to scene. Some scenes may fill you with gratitude, others with regret. Speak to God about this. You might pray for people with whom you interacted.
5. End with a prayer of thanksgiving for God's mercy and love. Ask him to refresh you as you sleep.

Guidelines for Pursuing Joy

Joy is not the result of changed circumstances, but of a heart that pursues joy. There is no formula for pursuing joy, but the following activities will help make the joy of the Lord more evident in your life. Consider each of these practices and write down your personal disciplines of joy.

PERSONAL JOURNEY: TO DO ON YOUR OWN

Knowledge is not what makes us unhurried or joyful people. We have to train—practice being who we want to become. Set aside some time to practice the disciplines of slowing down and celebration.

The Practice of Daily Solitude: Reviewing the Day with God

It can be difficult to carve out times of extended solitude, but every day you can practice solitude a few minutes at a time. Here's how:

1. Be still for a moment and quiet your mind.
2. Acknowledge that Jesus is present. Invite him to teach you.
3. Go back in your mind to when you first woke up and watch that scene, as if on video. This may lead you to pray for patience, greater love, courage, forgiveness, or other virtues.
4. Continue to reflect on the day, going from scene to scene. Some scenes may fill you with gratitude, others with regret. Speak to God about this. You might pray for people with whom you interacted.
5. End with a prayer of thanksgiving for God's mercy and love. Ask him to refresh you as you sleep.

Guidelines for Pursuing Joy

Joy is not the result of changed circumstances, but of a heart that pursues joy. There is no formula for pursuing joy, but the following activities will help make the joy of the Lord more evident in your life. Consider each of these practices and write down your personal disciplines of joy.

PERSONAL JOURNEY:
TO DO ON YOUR OWN

Knowledge is not what makes us unhurried or joyful people. We have to train—practice being who we want to become. Set aside some time to practice the disciplines of slowing down and celebration.

The Practice of Daily Solitude: Reviewing the Day with God

It can be difficult to carve out times of extended solitude, but every day you can practice solitude a few minutes at a time. Here's how:

1. Be still for a moment and quiet your mind.
2. Acknowledge that Jesus is present. Invite him to teach you.
3. Go back in your mind to when you first woke up and watch that scene, as if on video. This may lead you to pray for patience, greater love, courage, forgiveness, or other virtues.
4. Continue to reflect on the day, going from scene to scene. Some scenes may fill you with gratitude, others with regret. Speak to God about this. You might pray for people with whom you interacted.
5. End with a prayer of thanksgiving for God's mercy and love. Ask him to refresh you as you sleep.

Guidelines for Pursuing Joy

Joy is not the result of changed circumstances, but of a heart that pursues joy. There is no formula for pursuing joy, but the following activities will help make the joy of the Lord more evident in your life. Consider each of these practices and write down your personal disciplines of joy.

Disciplines of joy	Suggested activities	My joy disciplines
Practice the discipline of celebration.	Do activities that bring you pleasure — being with people you love, enjoying good food, etc., and reflecting on the God who has given you such wonderful gifts.	
Start pursuing joy *today*.	Psalm 118:24 tells us to rejoice and be glad in *this* day. If we wait until conditions are perfect, we won't rejoice at all.	
Find a "joy" mentor.	Intentionally spend time with life-enhancing, "joy-carrying," "joy-producing" people. Prize them. Thank them.	
Pray for joy.	Pray that the Holy Spirit will produce the fruit of joy in your life in greater abundance.	
Set aside one day a week to celebrate.	Eat foods you love, listen to music, surround yourself with beauty, etc. As you do these things, savor every moment and thank God for his wonderful goodness.	
Unplug the television for a week.	Instead of seeking "rest" in front of the television, nurture conversation with family and/or friends, think new thoughts, sleep more, read more, etc.	
Discipline your mind to view life from a biblical perspective.	To some degree, joy flows from a certain kind of thinking. How much more joy might you have if you viewed all events in light of Jesus' resurrection and his ultimate triumph?	

PLANNING NOTES

Disciplines of joy	Suggested activities	My joy disciplines
Practice the discipline of celebration.	Do activities that bring you pleasure — being with people you love, enjoying good food, etc., and reflecting on the God who has given you such wonderful gifts.	
Start pursuing joy *today*.	Psalm 118:24 tells us to rejoice and be glad in *this* day. If we wait until conditions are perfect, we won't rejoice at all.	
Find a "joy" mentor.	Intentionally spend time with life-enhancing, "joy-carrying," "joy-producing" people. Prize them. Thank them.	
Pray for joy.	Pray that the Holy Spirit will produce the fruit of joy in your life in greater abundance.	
Set aside one day a week to celebrate.	Eat foods you love, listen to music, surround yourself with beauty, etc. As you do these things, savor every moment and thank God for his wonderful goodness.	
Unplug the television for a week.	Instead of seeking "rest" in front of the television, nurture conversation with family and/or friends, think new thoughts, sleep more, read more, etc.	
Discipline your mind to view life from a biblical perspective.	To some degree, joy flows from a certain kind of thinking. How much more joy might you have if you viewed all events in light of Jesus' resurrection and his ultimate triumph?	

Disciplines of joy	Suggested activities	My joy disciplines
Practice the discipline of celebration.	Do activities that bring you pleasure — being with people you love, enjoying good food, etc., and reflecting on the God who has given you such wonderful gifts.	
Start pursuing joy *today*.	Psalm 118:24 tells us to rejoice and be glad in *this* day. If we wait until conditions are perfect, we won't rejoice at all.	
Find a "joy" mentor.	Intentionally spend time with life-enhancing, "joy-carrying," "joy-producing" people. Prize them. Thank them.	
Pray for joy.	Pray that the Holy Spirit will produce the fruit of joy in your life in greater abundance.	
Set aside one day a week to celebrate.	Eat foods you love, listen to music, surround yourself with beauty, etc. As you do these things, savor every moment and thank God for his wonderful goodness.	
Unplug the television for a week.	Instead of seeking "rest" in front of the television, nurture conversation with family and/or friends, think new thoughts, sleep more, read more, etc.	
Discipline your mind to view life from a biblical perspective.	To some degree, joy flows from a certain kind of thinking. How much more joy might you have if you viewed all events in light of Jesus' resurrection and his ultimate triumph?	

PLANNING NOTES

Planning a Time of Extended Solitude

In *The Life You've Always Wanted*, John Ortberg shared a plan for eight hours of solitude. Remember that this practice may not be easy for you. You may feel as if you are wasting your time because you are not *doing* something. Or you may feel intimidated, which is why the following structure may help you.

1. Find a place where you can be uninterrupted and alone, such as a park or retreat center.

2. Spend time the night before to prepare, to ask God to bless the day and to tell him that you want to devote the day to him. This day will be your gift to God, but even more, it is a gift God wants to give you. What do you need from him? A sense of healing and forgiveness? Conviction for an apathetic heart? Compassion? A renewed sense of mission? Ask God for this.

3. Arrange the day around listening to God. The following format is adapted from Glandion Carney's book *The Spiritual Formation Toolkit*.

8:00–9:00	Prepare your mind and heart, take a walk, or do whatever will help you set aside concerns over tasks and responsibilities. Try to arrange your morning so you can remain in silence from the time you awaken.
9:00–11:00	Read and meditate on Scripture, taking time to stop to reflect when God seems to be speaking to you through the text.
11:00–12:00	Write down responses to what you have read. Speak to God about them.
12:00–1:00	Eat lunch and take a walk, reflecting on the morning.
1:00–2:00	Take a nap.
2:00–3:00	Set goals that emerge from the day's reflection.
3:00–4:00	Write down three goals and other thoughts in a journal. You may want to do this in the form of a letter to God. Prepare to reenter society.

Planning a Time of Extended Solitude

In *The Life You've Always Wanted*, John Ortberg shared a plan for eight hours of solitude. Remember that this practice may not be easy for you. You may feel as if you are wasting your time because you are not *doing* something. Or you may feel intimidated, which is why the following structure may help you.

1. Find a place where you can be uninterrupted and alone, such as a park or retreat center.

2. Spend time the night before to prepare, to ask God to bless the day and to tell him that you want to devote the day to him. This day will be your gift to God, but even more, it is a gift God wants to give you. What do you need from him? A sense of healing and forgiveness? Conviction for an apathetic heart? Compassion? A renewed sense of mission? Ask God for this.

3. Arrange the day around listening to God. The following format is adapted from Glandion Carney's book *The Spiritual Formation Toolkit*.

8:00–9:00	Prepare your mind and heart, take a walk, or do whatever will help you set aside concerns over tasks and responsibilities. Try to arrange your morning so you can remain in silence from the time you awaken.
9:00–11:00	Read and meditate on Scripture, taking time to stop to reflect when God seems to be speaking to you through the text.
11:00–12:00	Write down responses to what you have read. Speak to God about them.
12:00–1:00	Eat lunch and take a walk, reflecting on the morning.
1:00–2:00	Take a nap.
2:00–3:00	Set goals that emerge from the day's reflection.
3:00–4:00	Write down three goals and other thoughts in a journal. You may want to do this in the form of a letter to God. Prepare to reenter society.

PLANNING NOTES

CLOSING MEDITATION

1 MINUTE

Dear God, life "outside the park" really is busy, and we all suffer the harmful effects of hurry sickness. Please help us to recognize its symptoms and take steps to slow down and focus our minds and hearts on you. Thank you for being a joyous God and for desiring us to experience the joy only you can give. Help us learn to recognize and celebrate "dee dah day" moments. Fill us with gratitude so that we thank you for each one of them. Fill us with your joy so that other people who don't yet know you will be drawn to you. Amen.

Praying and Confessing

BEFORE YOU LEAD
Synopsis

When people are desperate enough, they pray. Unfortunately, many people pray *only* when they are desperate, only when their resources and options have been exhausted. Part of the reason for this is that we tend to trust in ourselves more than in God and we aren't completely convinced that prayer makes a difference.

As you'll discover during this session, the Bible teaches that prayer is powerful. It changes things. When we pray, heaven listens. Prayer, perhaps more than any other activity, expresses the fact that God invites us to be in a personal relationship with him. Through prayer, our human hearts are knit together with the heart of God.

As essential as prayer is, however, it doesn't automatically flow out of us without effort or discipline—no matter how much we love God. Prayer is learned behavior. Even Jesus' disciples, who had been taught about prayer since their earliest days, asked him to teach them how to pray. Through this session, you'll guide participants in discovering some basic practices that will help them establish regular prayer times and make those times meaningful and effective.

This session will help participants feel more capable of learning how to pray. John Ortberg reminds us that when it comes to prayer, we're all beginners. So prayer is no place for heroics. No one can develop a lengthy, in-depth, meaningful, and effective prayer life overnight. Each of us needs to start right where we are, one step at a time.

God wants us to talk honestly with him about the concerns close to our hearts, but he also calls us to intercessory prayer—to pray boldly and persistently on behalf of other people. In *The Life You've Always Wanted* John Ortberg points out that history belongs to the intercessors—those who believe in the changing power of prayer and pray the future into being. He writes, "You don't know how many people have been strengthened because you asked God to encourage them; how many people have been healed because you prayed for their bodies; how many spiritual runaways have come home because you prayed for their souls."

Confession, the other spiritual discipline we'll explore in this session, goes hand in hand with prayer. The Bible reveals that each of us has sinned, which damages our relationship with God and others and prevents us from living the life we want to live. Confession opens the door to God's liberating forgiveness. We need to confess our sin not only to wipe away our guilt but in order to heal and become the transformed people we long to be. Confession is absolutely essential if our hearts are to be knit together with the heart of God.

Key Points of This Session

1. *Prayer is powerful, and when we pray all of heaven stops to listen.* God commands his people to pray. Prayer changes God's actions. Prayer knits our hearts with God's heart. Simple prayer is talking honestly to God about what is happening in our lives—about who we are and what is important to us, not about who we ought to be or what ought to concern us. Intercessory prayer is persistently approaching God about the needs of others.

2. *Prayer doesn't flow out of us without effort or discipline.* The practice of biblical prayer is learned behavior. Even Jesus' disciples, who had been taught about prayer since their earliest days, saw something different in the way Jesus prayed and asked him to teach them how to pray.

3. *The practice of confession opens the door to God's liberating forgiveness. It not only wipes away our guilt but enables us to become the transformed people we long to be.* Confession, a spiritual discipline that goes hand in hand with prayer, is absolutely essential if our hearts are to be knit together with the heart of God. Confession enables us to take appropriate responsibility for what we have done and to begin healing relationships that have been damaged by sin.

Suggested Reading

Chapters six and eight of *The Life You've Always Wanted*

SESSION OUTLINE

55 MINUTES

    I. Introduction (5 minutes)
       Welcome
       What's to Come
       Questions to Think About

    II. Video Presentation: "Praying and Confessing" (14 minutes)

    III. Group Discovery (29 minutes)
       Video Highlights (5 minutes)
       Large Group Exploration (10 minutes)
       Small Group Exploration (9 minutes)
       Group Discussion (5 minutes)

    IV. Personal Journey (6 minutes)

    V. Closing Meditation (1 minute)

Prayer, perhaps more than any other activity, is the concrete expression of the fact that we are invited into a relationship with God. . . . Confession is not primarily something God has us do because he needs it. . . . It is a practice that, done wisely, will help us become transformed.

—John Ortberg

Praying and Confessing

INTRODUCTION

5 MINUTES

Welcome

> Participant's Guide page 49.
>
> Welcome participants to *The Life You've Always Wanted* session three, "Praying and Confessing."

What's to Come

Many of us admit to having a rather weak prayer life. Often prayer is most important to us when we're desperate, when our resources and options have been exhausted and there's nothing left to do. The reason prayer isn't more important every day is simple: we tend to trust in ourselves more than in God and we aren't fully convinced that our prayers will change God's actions.

But the Bible teaches that our prayers matter. Today we're going to learn how to develop a more meaningful and effective prayer life. We'll also explore the discipline of confession, which liberates us from the guilt of our sin and helps transform us so we become more like Christ. Prayer and confession are essential if our hearts are to be knit together with the heart of God.

Praying and Confessing

SESSION THREE

Prayer, perhaps more than any other activity, is the concrete expression of the fact that we are invited into a relationship with God. . . . Confession is not primarily something God has us do because he needs it. . . . It is a practice that, done wisely, will help us become transformed.

—John Ortberg

49

PLANNING NOTES

Let's begin by considering a few questions related to prayer and confession. These questions are on page 50 of your Participant's Guide.

Questions to Think About

> Participant's Guide page 50.
>
> As time permits, ask participants to respond to two or more of the following questions.

1. What is your first response when you hear someone speak of the *discipline* of prayer?

   Responses will vary, but most people will be somewhat wary— or at least a bit afraid of falling asleep while praying! Most people feel their prayer life is inadequate, so the discipline of prayer sounds too hard. People often feel intimated, thinking they have to do what appears impossible in order to have a worthwhile prayer life.

2. What are some of the reasons people pray?

   Expect responses to vary considerably and include: do it because they feel obligated to, do it because they want God to accomplish something that they cannot, do it because they want to have a meaningful relationship with God, do it because they trust God enough to share what really concerns them, do it because they want to participate in what God is doing, do it to intercede for other people or circumstances, etc.

   Desperate
   "when all else fails
   pray!"

3. Describe times in your life when sin (and it doesn't have to be your sin) has affected your relationship with another person or with God.

   The point is, sin harms relationships. Our sin obviously hurts our relationship with God and our relationships with other people. It causes us to "hide," to be less than honest and not fully present in our relationships, and it may cause us to lash out at others. The sin of people far removed from us affects our relationships with God and with other people as well. The sin of an abusive parent, for example, is likely to affect a child's

QUESTIONS TO THINK ABOUT

1. What is your first response when you hear someone speak of the *discipline* of prayer?

2. What are some of the reasons people pray?

3. Describe times in your life when sin (and it doesn't have to be your sin) has affected your relationship with another person or with God.

4. When you hear the phrase "confess your sins to God," what comes to mind? Why?

PLANNING NOTES

relationships with foster or adoptive parents, with authority figures, with friends and siblings, with God, with a future spouse.

4. When you hear the phrase "confess your sins to God," what comes to mind? Why?

   No doubt participants will give different responses such as: not liking to confess their sins to God, how freeing confession to God can be, our need to be honest before God concerning our sins, our need to live holy lives, and wondering why we have to confess our sins to the God who already knows them.

Let's keep these ideas in mind as we view the video. There is space to take notes on page 51 of your Participant's Guide.

VIDEO PRESENTATION: "PRAYING AND CONFESSING"

14 MINUTES

Participant's Guide page 51.

Video Observations

Prayer really does matter

No heroics—start where you are

Pray about what really matters

Stains on the sofa

The real value of confession

50 • The Life You've Always Wanted Participant's Guide

QUESTIONS TO THINK ABOUT

1. What is your first response when you hear someone speak of the *discipline* of prayer?

2. What are some of the reasons people pray?

3. Describe times in your life when sin (and it doesn't have to be your sin) has affected your relationship with another person or with God.

4. When you hear the phrase "confess your sins to God," what comes to mind? Why?

Session Three: Praying and Confessing • 51

VIDEO OBSERVATIONS

Prayer really does matter

No heroics—start where you are

Pray about what really matters

Stains on the sofa

The real value of confession

PLANNING NOTES

GROUP DISCOVERY

⟨ **29** MINUTES ⟩

> **If your group has seven or more members,** use the Video Highlights with the entire group (5 minutes), then complete the Large Group Exploration (10 minutes), and break into small groups of three to five people for the Small Group Exploration (9 minutes). At the end, bring everyone together for the closing Group Discussion (5 minutes).
>
> **If your group has fewer than seven members,** begin with the Video Highlights (5 minutes), then complete both the Large Group Exploration (10 minutes) and the Small Group Exploration (9 minutes). Wrap up your discovery time with the Group Discussion (5 minutes).

Please turn to page 52 of your Participant's Guide.

Video Highlights • 5 minutes

> Participant's Guide page 52.
>
> As time permits, ask one or more of the following questions, which directly relate to the video the participants have just seen.

1. What is your response to the idea of praying five minutes a day, in the same place and at about the same time? In what ways would it be an effective (or ineffective) way to start building a time of regular prayer?

   SUGGESTED RESPONSE: *Although responses may differ, most participants will probably agree that "any time is better than no time" and that it's important to make prayer a priority. We can always pray longer at another time if we want to, but at least this way we are praying every day. Some participants may resist the idea of limiting their prayer time to five minutes.*

2. What has been your experience with the "monkeys jumping in the banana trees" when it comes to prayer? Why is it important to take time to settle down the "monkeys," and why is it important to pay attention if one "monkey" refuses to settle down?

VIDEO HIGHLIGHTS

1. What is your response to the idea of praying five minutes a day, in the same place and at about the same time? In what ways would it be an effective (or ineffective) way to start building a time of regular prayer?

2. What has been your experience with the "monkeys jumping in the banana trees" when it comes to prayer? Why is it important to take time to settle down the "monkeys," and why is it important to pay attention if one "monkey" refuses to settle down?

3. Why do we have to confess our sins to God?

PLANNING NOTES

Prayer is learned.

Bring the real, honest you.

Why confess?

It's for our sake.

It's how do I become a different person.

Pray to feel differently about a reoccurring sin.

SUGGESTED RESPONSE: *Expect a few chuckles as participants relate to this struggle. The "monkeys" can at times make it impossible to pray. At the same time, it is important to bring our real, honest selves before God and talk with him about what really matters to us. The monkey that won't settle down might be exactly what we need to talk to God about. If we pray too much about what we "ought" to pray about instead of what is on our heart, praying can seem irrelevant and cold, too practiced and routine. God longs to know us—just the way we are—and be known by us!*

3. Why do we have to confess our sins to God?

   SUGGESTED RESPONSE: *Sin is a barrier between us and our holy God. Confession helps us come to grips with the reality of our sin and sets us free to experience the fullness of God's forgiveness and love. The process of forgiveness changes us so that we become more aware of the "stains we put on the sofa" and have an increasing desire to not do them.*

Please turn to page 53 of your Participant's Guide, and we'll explore the power of prayer.

Large Group Exploration • 10 minutes

> Participant's Guide page 53.

The Power of Prayer

Usually we think of events on earth being interrupted because of actions in heaven. But our prayers are so important, so powerful, that all of heaven listens to our prayers—and God responds. Prayer is about more than changing the course of history, however. Prayer is about our relationship with God. Perhaps more than any other activity, prayer expresses the fact that God has invited us into a personal relationship with him. Through prayer our human hearts are knit together with the heart of God. So let's explore some of what the Bible says about prayer and its impact.

1. Genesis 18:20–33 presents a most interesting prayer dialogue between God and Abraham. What difference did Abraham's persistent requests make?

VIDEO HIGHLIGHTS

1. What is your response to the idea of praying five minutes a day, in the same place and at about the same time? In what ways would it be an effective (or ineffective) way to start building a time of regular prayer?

2. What has been your experience with the "monkeys jumping in the banana trees" when it comes to prayer? Why is it important to take time to settle down the "monkeys," and why is it important to pay attention if one "monkey" refuses to settle down?

3. Why do we have to confess our sins to God?

Session Three: Praying and Confessing • 53

LARGE GROUP EXPLORATION

The Power of Prayer

Usually we think of events on earth being interrupted because of actions in heaven. But our prayers are so important, so powerful, that all of heaven listens to our prayers—and God responds. Prayer is about more than changing the course of history, however. Prayer is about our relationship with God. Perhaps more than any other activity, prayer expresses the fact that God has invited us into a personal relationship with him. Through prayer our human hearts are knit together with the heart of God. So let's explore some of what the Bible says about prayer and its impact.

1. Genesis 18:20–33 presents a most interesting prayer dialogue between God and Abraham. What difference did Abraham's persistent requests make?

2. What do Psalm 34:15 and James 5:17–18 reveal about the effectiveness of prayer?

PLANNING NOTES

SUGGESTED RESPONSE: *God was prepared to destroy every person in Sodom because of the extent of their wickedness. Abraham, not without some concern for his own well-being, repeatedly approached God and asked for mercy because of the righteous people who might be living there. God agreed to alter his course because of Abraham's persistent requests.*

2. What do Psalm 34:15 and James 5:17–18 reveal about the effectiveness of prayer?

   SUGGESTED RESPONSE: *God listens to the prayers of righteous people, and their prayers change things. Elijah, who was just like us, prayed earnestly that it would not rain, and God kept it from raining for three and a half years. When Elijah later prayed for rain, it rained.*

3. Some people believe that if we really love God, powerful prayers will flow out of us without effort or discipline. What do Psalm 105:4, Colossians 4:2, and 1 Thessalonians 5:17–18 reveal that contradict this viewpoint?

   SUGGESTED RESPONSE: *It is God's will for us to pray continually—the psalmist says to "seek his face always"—and that requires discipline and effort. We are to* devote *ourselves to prayer, and that takes dedication. Prayer is work.*

4. How do we know God really wants us to ask him for help when we're in trouble? (See Psalm 10:17; Luke 18:7–8; Philippians 4:6.)

   SUGGESTED RESPONSE: *God cares about us and listens to our prayers when we are in trouble. He will quickly bring justice to his "chosen ones" who cry out to him when they are in need. He actually invites us to present our requests to him.*

5. How honest do you think we can afford to be in our prayers to God? (See Numbers 11:10–15.)

   SUGGESTED RESPONSE: *Moses was feeling overwhelmed when he prayed about the burden he had of caring for the Israelites, and he didn't hold anything back. He spoke frankly to God about all of the monkeys jumping around in the banana trees!*

LARGE GROUP EXPLORATION

The Power of Prayer

Usually we think of events on earth being interrupted because of actions in heaven. But our prayers are so important, so powerful, that all of heaven listens to our prayers—and God responds. Prayer is about more than changing the course of history, however. Prayer is about our relationship with God. Perhaps more than any other activity, prayer expresses the fact that God has invited us into a personal relationship with him. Through prayer our human hearts are knit together with the heart of God. So let's explore some of what the Bible says about prayer and its impact.

1. Genesis 18:20–33 presents a most interesting prayer dialogue between God and Abraham. What difference did Abraham's persistent requests make?

2. What do Psalm 34:15 and James 5:17–18 reveal about the effectiveness of prayer?

---

54 • The Life You've Always Wanted Participant's Guide

3. Some people believe that if we really love God, powerful prayers will flow out of us without effort or discipline. What do Psalm 105:4, Colossians 4:2, and 1 Thessalonians 5:17–18 reveal that contradict this viewpoint?

4. How do we know God really wants us to ask him for help when we're in trouble? (See Psalm 10:17; Luke 18:7–8; Philippians 4:6.)

5. How honest do you think we can afford to be in our prayers to God? (See Numbers 11:10–15.)

6. Many prayers of intercession are recorded in the Bible. Let's look at three examples of intercessory prayers and note what makes them powerful and effective.

Prayer	What makes it powerful and effective?
Nehemiah 1:4–11	
2 Samuel 5:17–25	
Colossians 1:9–12	

PLANNING NOTES

6. Many prayers of intercession are recorded in the Bible. Let's look at three examples of intercessory prayers and note what makes them powerful and effective.

Prayer	What makes it powerful and effective?
Nehemiah 1:4–11	*This is a deep, heart-felt prayer that comes from days of fasting and focusing on God's will. It is a bold but humble appeal to God's character and promises.*
2 Samuel 5:17–25	*These prayers, which led to great victories for Israel, are based on David's intimate relationship with God. David sought God's will for every move he made and listened for and obeyed the Lord's instructions.*
Colossians 1:9–12	*This commitment of long-term, fervent prayer for the Colossians was a result of Paul and Timothy's love for Christ and the gospel. Spiritual growth was dear to their hearts, so they prayed passionately for spiritual growth in other people.*

We will now break into groups of three to five to complete the Small Group Exploration, which begins on page 55. I will give you a one-minute notice before we rejoin for our Group Discussion.

Small Group Exploration • 9 minutes

Participant's Guide page 55.

Confession: Life Beyond Regret

Although we may not talk much about sin, all of us have sinned. Or, as John Ortberg pointed out in the video, we have all stained the sofa. The Bible clearly states that God freely forgives our sins, but many of us struggle to live in the reality of that forgiveness. That's why the practice of confession is necessary to our spiritual growth. Confession is not something God has us do because *he* needs it. Rather, confession is a practice that, done wisely, will help us become the transformed people we long to be. Let's explore what the Bible says about our sin and need for confession.

3. Some people believe that if we really love God, powerful prayers will flow out of us without effort or discipline. What do Psalm 105:4, Colossians 4:2, and 1 Thessalonians 5:17–18 reveal that contradict this viewpoint?

4. How do we know God really wants us to ask him for help when we're in trouble? (See Psalm 10:17; Luke 18:7–8; Philippians 4:6.)

5. How honest do you think we can afford to be in our prayers to God? (See Numbers 11:10–15.)

6. Many prayers of intercession are recorded in the Bible. Let's look at three examples of intercessory prayers and note what makes them powerful and effective.

Prayer	What makes it powerful and effective?
Nehemiah 1:4–11	
2 Samuel 5:17–25	
Colossians 1:9–12	

SMALL GROUP EXPLORATION

Confession: Life Beyond Regret

Although we may not talk much about sin, all of us have sinned. Or, as John Ortberg pointed out in the video, we have all stained the sofa. The Bible clearly states that God freely forgives our sins, but many of us struggle to live in the reality of that forgiveness. That's why the practice of confession is necessary to our spiritual growth. Confession is not something God has us do because *he* needs it. Rather, confession is a practice that, done wisely, will help us become the transformed people we long to be. Let's explore what the Bible says about our sin and need for confession.

1. Where did our "stain of sin" originate and what can be done about it? (See Romans 3:22–24; 5:12.)

PLANNING NOTES

1. Where did our "stain of sin" originate and what can be done about it? (See Romans 3:22–24; 5:12.)

   SUGGESTED RESPONSE: *The sins of the human race began with Adam and Eve. Since then, every person has been born with a sinful nature. Every one of us has sinned, but God makes us righteous through our faith in Jesus. We are justified freely through Christ's redemption.*

2. In story after story, the Bible exposes the consequences of having a sinful nature. Look up the following passages and write down the consequence of sin revealed in each.

Scripture	Consequence of a sinful nature
Proverbs 5:22–23	*Our sins ensnare us and hold us tightly in their grip. Sin leads to death because we are led astray by our own folly and lack of discipline.*
Jeremiah 5:25	*Our sins deprive us of God's goodness.*
John 8:34	*Sin enslaves us — we can't escape it.*
Romans 6:23	*Sin leads to death.*
Romans 8:7–8	*The sinful mind is set on fulfilling the desires of a sinful nature and is hostile to God. Those who are controlled by a sinful nature cannot please God.*
Galatians 5:19–21	*Sin bears the fruit of sexual immorality, impurity, debauchery, idolatry, witchcraft, hatred, discord, jealousy, fits of rage, selfish ambition, dissentions, factions, envy, drunkenness, orgies, etc., all of which deprive us of the kingdom of God.*
James 1:13–15	*We are tempted by our own evil desires, which lead to sin, which leads to death.*

3. One of the hazards of sin is that it distorts our ability to detect its presence.

   a. In what way(s) is this evident in the story of David and Bathsheba? (See 2 Samuel 11:1–9, 14–17; 12:1–7, 13.)

   SUGGESTED RESPONSE: *Scripture doesn't tell us all that David was thinking about when he committed these sins, but David had walked closely with God for a long time, so something clouded David's awareness of sin. Sin involves denial, as David clearly illustrates in his discussion with Nathan. David couldn't see his own sin, but became angry when Nathan told a parable illustrating what David had done.*

SMALL GROUP EXPLORATION

Session Three: Praying and Confessing • 55

Confession: Life Beyond Regret

Although we may not talk much about sin, all of us have sinned. Or, as John Ortberg pointed out in the video, we have all stained the sofa. The Bible clearly states that God freely forgives our sins, but many of us struggle to live in the reality of that forgiveness. That's why the practice of confession is necessary to our spiritual growth. Confession is not something God has us do because *he* needs it. Rather, confession is a practice that, done wisely, will help us become the transformed people we long to be. Let's explore what the Bible says about our sin and need for confession.

1. Where did our "stain of sin" originate and what can be done about it? (See Romans 3:22–24; 5:12.)

PLANNING NOTES

_____

_____

_____

_____

_____

_____

_____

_____

56 • The Life You've Always Wanted Participant's Guide

2. In story after story, the Bible exposes the consequences of having a sinful nature. Look up the following passages and write down the consequence of sin revealed in each.

Scripture	Consequence of a sinful nature
Proverbs 5:22–23	
Jeremiah 5:25	
John 8:34	
Romans 6:23	
Romans 8:7–8	
Galatians 5:19–21	
James 1:13–15	

Session Three: Praying and Confessing • 57

3. One of the hazards of sin is that it distorts our ability to detect its presence.

    a. In what way(s) is this evident in the story of David and Bathsheba? (See 2 Samuel 11:1–9, 14–17; 12:1–7, 13.)

    b. What did Jesus warn us about in Matthew 7:3–5? How does this teaching relate to David's situation? How does it relate to us?

Did You Know?

God uses many ways to convict us of our sin: dreams and words (Job 33:14–18), consequences (Luke 15:11–18; Psalm 107:10–12, 17–20), the gospel message (Acts 2:36–37), our consciences and guilt (John 8:3–9), the Holy Spirit (John 16:7–9), and his discipline (Hebrews 12:5–6).

b. What did Jesus warn us about in Matthew 7:3–5? How does this teaching relate to David's situation? How does it relate to us?

SUGGESTED RESPONSE: *Jesus warned his followers about the danger of being concerned about the sins of others while stubbornly overlooking their own sins. He told people to recognize their own sins first, before pointing out the sins of other people. In David's case, he could not see his own sin until it was revealed to him in the prophet Nathan's story. Jesus knew how easily we justify our sins. His warning reminds us how important it is to examine ourselves so we can deal appropriately with the sin that enslaves us.*

Did You Know?

God uses many ways to convict us of our sin: dreams and words (Job 33:14–18), consequences (Luke 15:11–18; Psalm 107:10–12, 17–20), the gospel message (Acts 2:36–37), our consciences and guilt (John 8:3–9), the Holy Spirit (John 16:7–9), and his discipline (Hebrews 12:5–6).

---

4. Knowing the full depth of our sinfulness, how does God respond to those who confess their sins to him? (See Isaiah 43:25; Joel 2:12–13; 1 John 1:7–9.)

SUGGESTED RESPONSE: *When we admit our sins and ask for God's forgiveness, he forgives and forgets them. He will be gracious, compassionate, slow to anger, and abounding in love when we "return" to him and confess our sins.*

5. What type of freedom do we experience when we confess our sins to God and turn away from them? (See Psalm 32:1–2; Acts 3:19; 2 Corinthians 7:10.)

SUGGESTED RESPONSE: *When we confess our sins, we not only receive God's forgiveness, we are blessed! He refreshes us! We can live without regret!*

3. One of the hazards of sin is that it distorts our ability to detect its presence.

   a. In what way(s) is this evident in the story of David and Bathsheba? (See 2 Samuel 11:1–9, 14–17; 12:1–7, 13.)

   b. What did Jesus warn us about in Matthew 7:3–5? How does this teaching relate to David's situation? How does it relate to us?

Did You Know?

God uses many ways to convict us of our sin: dreams and words (Job 33:14–18), consequences (Luke 15:11–18; Psalm 107:10–12, 17–20), the gospel message (Acts 2:36–37), our consciences and guilt (John 8:3–9), the Holy Spirit (John 16:7–9), and his discipline (Hebrews 12:5–6).

---

4. Knowing the full depth of our sinfulness, how does God respond to those who confess their sins to him? (See Isaiah 43:25; Joel 2:12–13; 1 John 1:7–9.)

5. What type of freedom do we experience when we confess our sins to God and turn away from them? (See Psalm 32:1–2; Acts 3:19; 2 Corinthians 7:10.)

6. What is it about confession, repentance, and forgiveness that enables us to face life with hope? (See Psalm 84:11–12; Romans 6:11–14.)

PLANNING NOTES

6. What is it about confession, repentance, and forgiveness that enables us to face life with hope? (See Psalm 84:11–12; Romans 6:11–14.)

SUGGESTED RESPONSE: *We are no longer slaves to sin. We can be "dead to sin" because of Jesus' shed blood. Sin no longer is our master. We can live a blameless and blessed life because of God's favor and honor.*

> Let participants know when one minute remains.
>
> When time is up, ask the groups to rejoin as one group.

Group Discussion • 5 minutes

> Participant's Guide page 59.
>
> As time permits, discuss the following questions that will help participants explore their understanding of the concepts covered in this session.

Now it's time for us to wrap up our discovery time. Please turn to page 59.

1. Based on this session, in what ways has your view of prayer changed? What have you learned that will help you practice a more disciplined prayer life? Which obstacles to prayer have you learned to overcome? What new hope do you have for your prayer life?

2. What impact does sin have on our lives—spiritually, emotionally, relationally—when we don't confess our sins to God? In what ways does sin harm our potential for spiritual growth?

3. Why is confession of our sins to God such an essential discipline? How have your views of confession changed as a result of what we've explored today?

4. Knowing the full depth of our sinfulness, how does God respond to those who confess their sins to him? (See Isaiah 43:25; Joel 2:12–13; 1 John 1:7–9.)

5. What type of freedom do we experience when we confess our sins to God and turn away from them? (See Psalm 32:1–2; Acts 3:19; 2 Corinthians 7:10.)

6. What is it about confession, repentance, and forgiveness that enables us to face life with hope? (See Psalm 84:11–12; Romans 6:11–14.)

GROUP DISCUSSION

1. Based on this session, in what ways has your view of prayer changed? What have you learned that will help you practice a more disciplined prayer life? Which obstacles to prayer have you learned to overcome? What new hope do you have for your prayer life?

2. What impact does sin have on our lives—spiritually, emotionally, relationally—when we don't confess our sins to God? In what ways does sin harm our potential for spiritual growth?

3. Why is confession of our sins to God such an essential discipline? How have your views of confession changed as a result of what we've explored today?

4. John Ortberg encourages us to each find someone with whom we can talk about the "stains we have put on the sofa," someone with whom we can share everything, even our gravest sins. What experience have you had with doing this? What encourages you to do this? What holds you back?

PLANNING NOTES

4. John Ortberg encourages us to each find someone with whom we can talk about the "stains we have put on the sofa," someone with whom we can share everything, even our gravest sins. What experience have you had with doing this? What encourages you to do this? What holds you back?

PERSONAL JOURNEY: TO DO NOW

6 MINUTES

Participant's Guide page 60.

Now let's turn to page 60 and spend a few minutes alone with God to review the key points and begin considering how the discipline of prayer and practice of confession can make a vital difference in our daily lives.

1. *Prayer is powerful, and when we pray all of heaven stops to listen.* God commands his people to pray. Prayer changes God's actions. Prayer knits our hearts with God's heart. Simple prayer is talking honestly to God about what is happening in our lives—about who we are and what is important to us, not about who we ought to be or what ought to concern us. Intercessory prayer is persistently approaching God about the needs of others.

How pleased are you with your prayer life?

In terms of your heart relationship with God?

In terms of what you talk with him about?

In terms of how you pray for others?

In terms of what your prayers accomplish?

Describe what you would like to see your prayer life become.

GROUP DISCUSSION

1. Based on this session, in what ways has your view of prayer changed? What have you learned that will help you practice a more disciplined prayer life? Which obstacles to prayer have you learned to overcome? What new hope do you have for your prayer life?

2. What impact does sin have on our lives—spiritually, emotionally, relationally—when we don't confess our sins to God? In what ways does sin harm our potential for spiritual growth?

3. Why is confession of our sins to God such an essential discipline? How have your views of confession changed as a result of what we've explored today?

4. John Ortberg encourages us to each find someone with whom we can talk about the "stains we have put on the sofa," someone with whom we can share everything, even our gravest sins. What experience have you had with doing this? What encourages you to do this? What holds you back?

PLANNING NOTES

PERSONAL JOURNEY: TO DO NOW

1. *Prayer is powerful, and when we pray all of heaven stops to listen.* God commands his people to pray. Prayer changes God's actions. Prayer knits our hearts with God's heart. Simple prayer is talking honestly to God about what is happening in our lives—about who we are and what is important to us, not about who we ought to be or what ought to concern us. Intercessory prayer is persistently approaching God about the needs of others.

   How pleased are you with your prayer life?

   In terms of your heart relationship with God?

   In terms of what you talk with him about?

   In terms of how you pray for others?

   In terms of what your prayers accomplish?

Describe what you would like to see your prayer life become.

2. *Prayer doesn't flow out of us without effort or discipline.* The practice of biblical prayer is learned behavior. Even Jesus' disciples, who had been taught about prayer since their earliest days, saw something different in the way Jesus prayed and asked him to teach them how to pray.

   What changes would you like to make in your prayer life, starting today?

   Which step(s) presented in this session can you take to begin building a more disciplined prayer time? For example, if you are not already doing so, are you willing to pray five minutes every day?

2. *Prayer doesn't flow out of us without effort or discipline.* The practice of biblical prayer is learned behavior. Even Jesus' disciples, who had been taught about prayer since their earliest days, saw something different in the way Jesus prayed and asked him to teach them how to pray.

What changes would you like to make in your prayer life, starting today?

Which step(s) presented in this session can you take to begin building a more disciplined prayer time? For example, if you are not already doing so, are you willing to pray five minutes every day?

3. *The practice of confession opens the door to God's liberating forgiveness. It not only wipes away our guilt but enables us to become the transformed people we long to be.* Confession, a spiritual discipline that goes hand in hand with prayer, is absolutely essential if our hearts are to be knit together with the heart of God. Confession enables us to take appropriate responsibility for what we have done and to begin healing relationships that have been damaged by sin.

Is the discipline of confessing your sins to God a regular part of your life? Why or why not?

What changes might you want to make in this area?

In what way(s) might unconfessed sin be affecting your life and the lives of people around you?

Let participants know when there is one minute remaining.

When time is up, remind participants that they may want to continue their journey on their own time by completing the exercise on pages 63–66 of their Participant's Guide. Then end the session with the Closing Meditation.

Describe what you would like to see your prayer life become.

2. *Prayer doesn't flow out of us without effort or discipline.* The practice of biblical prayer is learned behavior. Even Jesus' disciples, who had been taught about prayer since their earliest days, saw something different in the way Jesus prayed and asked him to teach them how to pray.

What changes would you like to make in your prayer life, starting today?

Which step(s) presented in this session can you take to begin building a more disciplined prayer time? For example, if you are not already doing so, are you willing to pray five minutes every day?

PLANNING NOTES

_____

_____

_____

_____

_____

_____

_____

_____

3. *The practice of confession opens the door to God's liberating forgiveness. It not only wipes away our guilt but enables us to become the transformed people we long to be.* Confession, a spiritual discipline that goes hand in hand with prayer, is absolutely essential if our hearts are to be knit together with the heart of God. Confession enables us to take appropriate responsibility for what we have done and to begin healing relationships that have been damaged by sin.

Is the discipline of confessing your sins to God a regular part of your life? Why or why not?

What changes might you want to make in this area?

In what way(s) might unconfessed sin be affecting your life and the lives of people around you?

PERSONAL JOURNEY: TO DO ON YOUR OWN

Establish a Prayer Pattern That Works for You

Read through the following tips for starting a regular prayer time. When you have finished, develop a prayer plan that works for you and begin to follow it. Make revisions as needed.

Tips on Starting a Regular Prayer Time

- *Keep your prayer time short.* Many people feel guilty about not praying and resolve to change their prayer habits. So they try to pray for far longer stretches of time than they are capable of doing. When they can't sustain long prayers, they give up until they feel guilty again. To avoid this cycle, keep your prayer time to five minutes every day at the same time, then pray more as you desire to do so.
- *Make your prayer time meaningful.* If beauty is important to you, pray outside or near a window with a view. Or light a candle to remind you that the light of God's presence and wisdom is available to guide you. Or pull up another chair to remind yourself that Jesus really is present with you. Use physical symbols such as these to support your practice of prayer.
- *Prepare ahead for your prayer time.* Before you pray, set aside a few minutes to settle your thoughts. You might take a few deep breaths and allow your mind to slow down. You might focus your eyes on a physical object or whisper "Heavenly Father" a few times until your mind quiets.
- *Pray about what is on your heart, not what you wish was on your heart.* Come before God as you are, opening your heart and making your requests to him. Avoid praying about the "right things" that you don't especially care about.
- *Learn to be fully present when you pray.* It's easy for our minds to wander when we pray. If your mind keeps returning to a particular thought, event, or person during prayer, it may indicate that you need to talk with God about the matter. During your prayer times, speak with God about what really concerns you.

PERSONAL JOURNEY: TO DO ON YOUR OWN

Establish a Prayer Pattern That Works for You

Read through the following tips for starting a regular prayer time. When you have finished, develop a prayer plan that works for you and begin to follow it. Make revisions as needed.

Tips on Starting a Regular Prayer Time

- *Keep your prayer time short.* Many people feel guilty about not praying and resolve to change their prayer habits. So they try to pray for far longer stretches of time than they are capable of doing. When they can't sustain long prayers, they give up until they feel guilty again. To avoid this cycle, keep your prayer time to five minutes every day at the same time, then pray more as you desire to do so.

- *Make your prayer time meaningful.* If beauty is important to you, pray outside or near a window with a view. Or light a candle to remind you that the light of God's presence and wisdom is available to guide you. Or pull up another chair to remind yourself that Jesus really is present with you. Use physical symbols such as these to support your practice of prayer.

- *Prepare ahead for your prayer time.* Before you pray, set aside a few minutes to settle your thoughts. You might take a few deep breaths and allow your mind to slow down. You might focus your eyes on a physical object or whisper "Heavenly Father" a few times until your mind quiets.

- *Pray about what is on your heart, not what you wish was on your heart.* Come before God as you are, opening your heart and making your requests to him. Avoid praying about the "right things" that you don't especially care about.

- *Learn to be fully present when you pray.* It's easy for our minds to wander when we pray. If your mind keeps returning to a particular thought, event, or person during prayer, it may indicate that you need to talk with God about the matter. During your prayer times, speak with God about what really concerns you.

My Personal Prayer Plan

What time of day is the best for me to set aside exclusively for prayer?

Where is the best place for me to pray at that time?

What is necessary for me to do to prepare my heart for prayer?

PERSONAL JOURNEY:
TO DO ON YOUR OWN

Establish a Prayer Pattern That Works for You

Read through the following tips for starting a regular prayer time. When you have finished, develop a prayer plan that works for you and begin to follow it. Make revisions as needed.

Tips on Starting a Regular Prayer Time

- *Keep your prayer time short.* Many people feel guilty about not praying and resolve to change their prayer habits. So they try to pray for far longer stretches of time than they are capable of doing. When they can't sustain long prayers, they give up until they feel guilty again. To avoid this cycle, keep your prayer time to five minutes every day at the same time, then pray more as you desire to do so.
- *Make your prayer time meaningful.* If beauty is important to you, pray outside or near a window with a view. Or light a candle to remind you that the light of God's presence and wisdom is available to guide you. Or pull up another chair to remind yourself that Jesus really is present with you. Use physical symbols such as these to support your practice of prayer.
- *Prepare ahead for your prayer time.* Before you pray, set aside a few minutes to settle your thoughts. You might take a few deep breaths and allow your mind to slow down. You might focus your eyes on a physical object or whisper "Heavenly Father" a few times until your mind quiets.
- *Pray about what is on your heart, not what you wish was on your heart.* Come before God as you are, opening your heart and making your requests to him. Avoid praying about the "right things" that you don't especially care about.
- *Learn to be fully present when you pray.* It's easy for our minds to wander when we pray. If your mind keeps returning to a particular thought, event, or person during prayer, it may indicate that you need to talk with God about the matter. During your prayer times, speak with God about what really concerns you.

My Personal Prayer Plan

What time of day is the best for me to set aside exclusively for prayer?

Where is the best place for me to pray at that time?

What is necessary for me to do to prepare my heart for prayer?

What will help me maintain my focus during my prayer time?

How will I decide what to pray about? (For example, you could make a list, or pray for what is most important to you at the time, etc.)

PLANNING NOTES

_____
_____
_____
_____
_____
_____
_____
_____
_____
_____
_____
_____
_____
_____
_____
_____
_____
_____
_____

What will help me maintain my focus during my prayer time?

How will I decide what to pray about? (For example, you could make a list, or pray for what is most important to you at the time, etc.)

A Six-Step Process for Spiritual Stain Removal

Carefully review the process of confession below, which John Ortberg shares in *The Life You've Always Wanted*. As you read, think of how you can apply these steps in your life and the positive difference they will make. Then begin applying them soon.

Preparation	We place ourselves under the care and guidance of the Holy Spirit. Without God's help, we tend toward self-condemnation for things we ought not to feel guilty about or gloss over ugly stains that need attention.
Self-examination	We reflect on our thoughts, words, and deeds. We examine our hearts in light of sin, such as the seven deadly sins (pride, anger, lust, envy, greed, sloth, and gluttony), or in light of the teachings of other Scripture, perhaps the Ten Commandments (Exodus 20) or the Beatitudes (Matthew 5). We honestly (and fearlessly) ask ourselves where we stand in regard to each of these. Then we take appropriate responsibility for our sinful choices and actions.
Perception	All sin involves denial and distorts our ability to detect its presence. So we need to see our sins through the eyes of God and through the eyes of anyone we have sinned against.
Ask *why?* And *what happened?*	Sin is often an attempt to meet a legitimate need in an illegitimate way. If we don't address that need appropriately, we'll keep sinning. So we need to ask ourselves why we pursued the course we took. We also need to face what happened as a result of our sin. True confession involves entering into the pain of anyone we've hurt and entering into God's pain over sin. Facing the consequences of our sin helps us develop a contrite heart that truly desires not to sin in that way again.
Make a new promise	Confession is not just naming sins we have done in the past. It involves our intentions about the future — a kind of promise. It involves a deep desire not to do these hurtful things again and an attempt to set right what we did wrong. It involves a resolution that, with God's help, we will change.
Healing grace	Grace is the final step in confession. God's grace allows the burden of our sin to cause pain and hardship in our lives. But as God's work is done in our hearts, God's grace also will completely release us from these burdens.

My Personal Prayer Plan

What time of day is the best for me to set aside exclusively for prayer?

Where is the best place for me to pray at that time?

What is necessary for me to do to prepare my heart for prayer?

What will help me maintain my focus during my prayer time?

How will I decide what to pray about? (For example, you could make a list, or pray for what is most important to you at the time, etc.)

PLANNING NOTES

A Six-Step Process for Spiritual Stain Removal

Carefully review the process of confession below, which John Ortberg shares in *The Life You've Always Wanted*. As you read, think of how you can apply these steps in your life and the positive difference they will make. Then begin applying them soon.

Preparation	We place ourselves under the care and guidance of the Holy Spirit. Without God's help, we either tend toward self-condemnation for things we ought not to feel guilty about or gloss over ugly stains that need attention.
Self-examination	We reflect on our thoughts, words, and deeds. We examine our hearts in light of sin, such as the seven deadly sins (pride, anger, lust, envy, greed, sloth, and gluttony), or in light of the teachings of other Scripture, perhaps the Ten Commandments (Exodus 20) or the Beatitudes (Matthew 5). We honestly (and fearlessly) ask ourselves where we stand in regard to each of these. Then we take appropriate responsibility for our sinful choices and actions.
Perception	All sin involves denial and distorts our ability to detect its presence. So we need to see our sins through the eyes of God and through the eyes of anyone we have sinned against.
Ask *why?* And *what* happened?	Sin is often an attempt to meet a legitimate need in an illegitimate way. If we don't address that need appropriately, we'll keep sinning. So we need to ask ourselves why we pursued the course we took. We also need to face what happened as a result of our

---

	sin. True confession involves entering into the pain of anyone we've hurt and entering into God's pain over sin. Facing the consequences of our sin helps us develop a contrite heart that truly desires not to sin in that way again.
Make a new promise	Confession is not just naming sins we have done in the past. It involves our intentions about the future — a kind of promise. It involves a deep desire not to do these hurtful things again and an attempt to set right what we did wrong. It involves a resolution that, with God's help, we will change.
Healing grace	Grace is the final step in confession. God's grace allows the burden of our sin to cause pain and hardship in our lives. But as God's work is done in our hearts, God's grace also will completely release us from these burdens.

CLOSING MEDITATION

> **1** MINUTE

Dear God, thank you for reminding us about the importance of prayer and confession, and for loving us so much that you long to be in vibrant relationship with us. Help us to apply what we've discovered during this session, to develop more focused prayer times and times of confession. Help us to learn to pray as you have taught us:

Our Father in heaven,
Hallowed be your name,
Your kingdom come,
Your will be done on earth as it is in heaven.
Give us today our daily bread.
Forgive us our debts,
As we also have forgiven our debtors.
And lead us not into temptation,
But deliver us from the evil one.
Amen.

Meditating on Scripture
and Seeking Guidance

BEFORE YOU LEAD
Synopsis

During this session you'll guide participants in discovering the key role the practice of biblical meditation plays in spiritual transformation. You'll also help them learn how to be receptive and responsive to the guidance of the Holy Spirit.

God commands his followers to focus on one thing in life: pursuit of God's kingdom and his righteousness above all else. But as much as we desire to be transformed into people who have that focus, it's not an easy process. We struggle with divided loyalties—what the Bible calls double-mindedness. Part of us desires intimacy with God while another part of us flees from it. Part of us wants to forgive while another part of us wants to hold a grudge. Our lack of focus on the one thing God commands results in minds and hearts that are cluttered with impurities—false beliefs, attitudes, deadly feelings, and misguided efforts—that lead us to sin and despair.

The solution to the clutter and conflict is found in James 4:8: "Wash your hands, you sinners, and purify your hearts, you double-minded." James was not writing about an ordinary cleansing, however. He referred to the cleansing that comes as our minds and hearts are immersed in the transforming power of God's Word, which occurs when we read and meditate on the Scriptures. This practice of biblical meditation is indispensable to spiritual growth. In *The Life You've Always Wanted,* John Ortberg writes that he has "never known someone leading a spiritually transformed life who had not been deeply saturated in Scripture."

In addition to the practice of meditating on Scripture, those who desire spiritual growth must learn to seek and respond to the Holy Spirit's guidance, which is available to everyone who wants to live a fruitful life for the kingdom of God. You'll guide participants in exploring how God spoke to people in the Old Testament and in learning how to listen for the Holy Spirit's "leadings" or "promptings" in their daily lives.

Contrary to what some people may think, seeking God's guidance is not being passive and letting circumstances dictate our direction. Nor is it a last-minute shortcut to decision making. Seeking God's guidance includes praying, exercising judgment, seeking wisdom, and taking initiative and responsibility. Pursuing the Holy Spirit's guidance means listening for the Spirit continually and being relentlessly responsive to the Spirit's leading so we learn how to live as Jesus would live if he were in our place.

Key Points of This Session

1. *God calls us to one thing in life—to pursue God's kingdom and his righteousness above all else.* The problem is, we tend to be double-minded: we want to do one thing but do or say the opposite. The practice of biblical meditation penetrates, cleanses, and transforms our hearts and minds, teaching us how to live fruitful lives for the kingdom of God. As we immerse ourselves in Scripture, we are transformed from double-mindedness to the single focus of pursuing God's kingdom.

2. *We need the Holy Spirit's guidance in order to discover how to live as Jesus would live if he were in our place.* The guidance of the Holy Spirit is not reserved for "important," "spiritually mature," or "more spiritual" people; it is available to each of us. The Holy Spirit can and will provide guidance when we seek the kingdom of God above all else. Learning to be receptive and responsive to the leadings or promptings of the Holy Spirit is nonoptional if we are to live transformed lives.

3. *Seeking God's guidance is an intentional choice. It is not a passive avoidance of responsibility, a shortcut to making decisions, or a way to escape risk.* Seeking God's guidance involves prayer, wisdom and discernment, initiative, choice, and responsibility. To seek God's guidance means learning to listen for the Spirit in all things and to be relentlessly responsive to pursuing God's will. God guides us not so we will perform the right actions but so we will learn how to become the right kind of people, so we will learn how to live in the context of seeking his kingdom.

Suggested Reading

Chapters nine and eleven of *The Life You've Always Wanted*

SESSION OUTLINE

55 MINUTES

I. Introduction (6 minutes)
Welcome
What's to Come
Questions to Think About

II. Video Presentation: "Meditating on Scripture and Seeking Guidance" (10 minutes)

III. Group Discovery (32 minutes)
Video Highlights (5 minutes)
Large Group Exploration (11 minutes)
Small Group Exploration (10 minutes)
Group Discussion (6 minutes)

IV. Personal Journey (6 minutes)

V. Closing Meditation (1 minute)

God's purpose in guidance is not to get us to perform the right actions. His purpose is to help us become the right kind of people.

—John Ortberg

Becoming vs. Doing

Meditating on Scripture and Seeking Guidance

INTRODUCTION

6 MINUTES

Welcome

> Participant's Guide page 67.
>
> Welcome participants to *The Life You've Always Wanted* session four, "Meditating on Scripture and Seeking Guidance."

What's to Come

During this session we will explore how we become single-minded people who pursue the one thing God wants us to pursue in life. We'll find out how to seek God's guidance for our lives. We'll discover that finding God's will isn't a passive "wait and see" approach. It is not an escape from responsibility or a shortcut to decision making. Finding God's will involves learning how to listen to the Holy Spirit's guidance and responding to it. We'll also find out why it is important—indeed essential—to meditate on Scripture, and how Scripture transforms us into single-minded people who live as Jesus would live if he were in our place.

Let's begin by considering a few questions related to seeking God's guidance as we pursue his kingdom. These questions are on page 68 of your Participant's Guide.

Meditating on Scripture and Seeking Guidance

SESSION FOUR

God's purpose in guidance is not to get us to perform the right actions. His purpose is to help us become the right kind of people.

—John Ortberg

67

---

68 • The Life You've Always Wanted Participant's Guide

QUESTIONS TO THINK ABOUT

1. What is your response when a person says God told him or her to do something? Do you believe the Holy Spirit leads, guides, or directs ordinary people today? Explain your answer.

2. Describe a time in your life when you felt that God was communicating something to you. How did you know it was God?

3. What is the difference between meditating on Scripture and reading the Bible in order to gain more knowledge?

4. What does God really want his followers to do?

PLANNING NOTES

Questions to Think About

> Participant's Guide page 68.
>
> As time permits, ask participants to respond to two or more of the following questions.

1. What is your response when a person says God told him or her to do something? Do you believe the Holy Spirit leads, guides, or directs ordinary people today? Explain your answer.

    Although participants will learn through this session that the Holy Spirit does guide people today, the objective of this question is to help participants identify their current beliefs and experiences. Some participants may respond positively when someone makes such a remark; others may be somewhat to very skeptical. It's important that participants identify whether or not their perceptions and beliefs are based on their opinion, comfort level, personal experiences, or what the Bible says.

2. Describe a time in your life when you felt that God was communicating something to you. How did you know it was God?

    Responses will vary and may include a realization that a particular thought was being impressed on their mind, having a specific feeling or desire, finding words of Scripture that seemed to speak specifically to them, seeing the results of the action they felt led to take, etc.

3. What is the difference between meditating on Scripture and reading the Bible in order to gain more knowledge?

    Some participants may have a clear understanding of this vital difference; others may not. By discussing this question, participants should realize that it is possible to read volumes of Scripture or gain biblical knowledge without actually allowing God to speak to us through his Word. To meditate on a Bible passage is to seek to allow the meaning of the passage to influence us. When we meditate, we anticipate that God will speak to us through his Word. We meditate not so much to gain knowledge, but to gain understanding.

QUESTIONS TO THINK ABOUT

1. What is your response when a person says God told him or her to do something? Do you believe the Holy Spirit leads, guides, or directs ordinary people today? Explain your answer.

2. Describe a time in your life when you felt that God was communicating something to you. How did you know it was God?

3. What is the difference between meditating on Scripture and reading the Bible in order to gain more knowledge?

4. What does God really want his followers to do?

PLANNING NOTES

4. What does God really want his followers to do?

    Expect varied responses, among them: evangelize, love God, pursue his kingdom, train themselves for service, care for the poor and infirm. See if your group can come to a consensus. This exercise itself may illustrate a lack of single-mindedness!

Let's keep these ideas in mind as we view the video. There is space to take notes on page 69 of your Participant's Guide.

VIDEO PRESENTATION:

"MEDITATING ON SCRIPTURE AND SEEKING GUIDANCE"

10 MINUTES

Participant's Guide page 69.

Video Observations

Obstacles to transformation

Passivity

Double-mindedness

Washing our minds with Scripture

The work of seeking guidance

QUESTIONS TO THINK ABOUT

1. What is your response when a person says God told him or her to do something? Do you believe the Holy Spirit leads, guides, or directs ordinary people today? Explain your answer.

2. Describe a time in your life when you felt that God was communicating something to you. How did you know it was God?

3. What is the difference between meditating on Scripture and reading the Bible in order to gain more knowledge?

4. What does God really want his followers to do?

VIDEO OBSERVATIONS

Obstacles to transformation

Passivity

Double-mindedness

Washing our minds with Scripture

The work of seeking guidance

PLANNING NOTES

GROUP DISCOVERY

32 MINUTES

> **If your group has seven or more members,** use the Video Highlights with the entire group (5 minutes), then complete the Large Group Exploration (11 minutes), and break into small groups of three to five people for the Small Group Exploration (10 minutes). At the end, bring everyone together for the closing Group Discussion (6 minutes).
>
> **If your group has fewer than seven members,** begin with the Video Highlights (5 minutes), then complete both the Large Group Exploration (11 minutes) and the Small Group Exploration (10 minutes). Wrap up your discovery time with the Group Discussion (6 minutes).

Please turn to page 70 of your Participant's Guide.

Video Highlights • 5 minutes

> Participant's Guide page 70.
>
> As time permits, ask one or more of the following questions, which directly relate to the video the participants have just seen.

[handwritten: You can't serve both God and mammon (worldly stuff),]

1. Now that we have a vivid image of double-mindedness in focus, what is double-mindedness? What is its source? And what impact does it have on our spiritual growth?

   SUGGESTED RESPONSE: *Double-mindedness means having divided loyalties. It comes from the spiritual battle we all face between seeking God or choosing sin. We want to pursue God, for example, but also want to live life our own way. We want to be generous with money, yet keep it for ourselves. When we are double-minded, we will have no more success in going where we want to go spiritually than the men in the canoe would have had arriving at a specific destination.*

VIDEO HIGHLIGHTS

1. Now that we have a vivid image of double-mindedness in focus, what is double-mindedness? What is its source? And what impact does it have on our spiritual growth?

2. If we can't "override" double-mindedness by willpower or by trying to do better, how can our tendency toward double-mindedness be changed?

3. In what way is passivity an obstacle to guidance and spiritual growth?

4. John Ortberg said that God guides us in ways that are consistent with Scripture and consistent with the person he has created each of us to be. Why is it important for us to remember these principles?

PLANNING NOTES

2. If we can't "override" double-mindedness by willpower or by trying to do better, how can our tendency toward double-mindedness be changed?

SUGGESTED RESPONSE: *Eliminating double-mindedness is not something we can do on our own, no matter how hard we try. It results from the power of the Holy Spirit at work in our lives. Double-mindedness is eliminated as our minds and hearts are cleansed by the "washing with water" through God's Word. This means that as we meditate on Scripture, as we immerse ourselves in it, our minds and hearts are "re-formed" and we become transformed into the kind of people who live as Jesus would live if he were in our place.*

3. In what way is passivity an obstacle to guidance and spiritual growth?

SUGGESTED RESPONSE: *Although some people believe pursuing God's will means doing nothing and allowing circumstances to dictate what happens, Scripture teaches that God really does guide us. And God wants us to actively pursue his will. If we don't actively seek God's guidance, we won't learn to discern his voice and we won't get to know him as we should.*

4. John Ortberg said that God guides us in ways that are consistent with the Scriptures and consistent with the person he has created each of us to be. Why is it important for us to remember these principles?

SUGGESTED RESPONSE: *The Bible provides "anchor points" to which we can compare what we discern God's guidance to be. His guidance will never contradict Scripture, and we need to rely on Scripture as well as on other sources of God's guidance. We also know that God guides us in ways that are consistent with our gifts. Although he may put us in situations that "stretch" us, knowing our gifts can help us verify God's will for us.*

We allow our desires to become God's will.

Please turn to page 71 of your Participant's Guide, and we will explore how God uses his Word to transform our minds and release us from double-mindedness.

VIDEO HIGHLIGHTS

1. Now that we have a vivid image of double-mindedness in focus, what is double-mindedness? What is its source? And what impact does it have on our spiritual growth?

2. If we can't "override" double-mindedness by willpower or by trying to do better, how can our tendency toward double-mindedness be changed?

3. In what way is passivity an obstacle to guidance and spiritual growth?

4. John Ortberg said that God guides us in ways that are consistent with Scripture and consistent with the person he has created each of us to be. Why is it important for us to remember these principles?

LARGE GROUP EXPLORATION

Double-Mindedness: Enemy of the One Important Thing

In *The Life You've Always Wanted,* John Ortberg wrote about the importance of pursuing "one thing" in life. When we pursue one thing, we have a singleness of purpose, a clarity of commitment, and a consistency in our choices. Jesus calls his followers to pursue one thing in life—to seek his kingdom and his righteousness above all else. That one thing ought to dominate our thoughts, choices, and deeds.

But most of us have divided loyalties. We live one moment in the pursuit of God's kingdom and the next moment in the pursuit of our own desires. We want to do one thing, but do or say the opposite. To put it simply, we are double-minded. And double-mindedness prevents us from living the life we want to live. So let's see how we can eliminate double-mindedness from our lives.

1. What is the one important thing Jesus commanded his followers to do? (See Matthew 6:33.)

2. What cautions and principles do we find in Scripture concerning our allegiance to and focus on the things of this world versus the things of God? (See Matthew 4:8–10; 6:24; Colossians 3:2; Titus 2:11–14.)

PLANNING NOTES

Large Group Exploration • *11 minutes*

Participant's Guide page 71.

Double-Mindedness: Enemy of the One Important Thing

In *The Life You've Always Wanted,* John Ortberg wrote about the importance of pursuing "one thing" in life. When we pursue one thing, we have a singleness of purpose, a clarity of commitment, and a consistency in our choices. Jesus calls his followers to pursue one thing in life—to seek his kingdom and his righteousness above all else. That one thing ought to dominate our thoughts, choices, and deeds.

But most of us have divided loyalties. We live one moment in the pursuit of God's kingdom and the next moment in the pursuit of our own desires. We want to do one thing, but do or say the opposite. To put it simply, we are double-minded. And double-mindedness prevents us from living the life we want to live. So let's see how we can eliminate double-mindedness from our lives.

1. What is the one important thing Jesus commanded his followers to do? (See Matthew 6:33.)

   SUGGESTED RESPONSE: *Jesus commanded his disciples (and us) to seek first the kingdom of God and his righteousness. This pursuit is the most important of all!*

2. What cautions and principles do we find in Scripture concerning our allegiance to and focus on the things of this world versus the things of God? (See Matthew 4:8–10, 6:24; Colossians 3:2; Titus 2:11–14.)

   SUGGESTED RESPONSE: *When Satan tried to bribe Jesus to worship him, Jesus said that we are to worship and serve God only, which clearly is in opposition to double-mindedness. Jesus told people they couldn't serve two masters (God and money were the specific ones he mentioned); they could serve only one. The apostle Paul told his readers to keep their minds focused on heavenly things, not earthly things. He encouraged them to live "self-controlled, upright and godly lives" while they focused their hope on*

LARGE GROUP EXPLORATION

Double-Mindedness: Enemy of the One Important Thing

In *The Life You've Always Wanted,* John Ortberg wrote about the importance of pursuing "one thing" in life. When we pursue one thing, we have a singleness of purpose, a clarity of commitment, and a consistency in our choices. Jesus calls his followers to pursue one thing in life—to seek his kingdom and his righteousness above all else. That one thing ought to dominate our thoughts, choices, and deeds.

But most of us have divided loyalties. We live one moment in the pursuit of God's kingdom and the next moment in the pursuit of our own desires. We want to do one thing, but do or say the opposite. To put it simply, we are double-minded. And double-mindedness prevents us from living the life we want to live. So let's see how we can eliminate double-mindedness from our lives.

1. What is the one important thing Jesus commanded his followers to do? (See Matthew 6:33.)

2. What cautions and principles do we find in Scripture concerning our allegiance to and focus on the things of this world versus the things of God? (See Matthew 4:8–10; 6:24; Colossians 3:2; Titus 2:11–14.)

PLANNING NOTES

God's kingdom. He reminded them that Jesus came to redeem and purify his people from all wickedness.

3. What do James 1:5–8 and 4:7–8 reveal about double-mindedness as an obstacle to seeking God's guidance and experiencing spiritual growth?

    SUGGESTED RESPONSE: *God gives wisdom generously to those who serve him. But a double-minded person is unstable in all he or she does and should not expect to receive wisdom from God. In fact, God tells double-minded people to confess their sins and "purify" their hearts. A double-minded person fails to make an ultimate commitment to God and his kingdom.*

4. The apostle Paul gives a great explanation of the nature of spiritual double-mindedness in Romans 7:18–24. What does he seem to think is the cause of double-mindedness, and what does he think he can do about it?

    SUGGESTED RESPONSE: *Paul gives a clear picture of the battle between good and evil that rages within him. He attributes the battle to his sinful nature and recognizes that he can't rescue himself from it.*

5. Some people think the battle of double-mindedness versus single-mindedness is a result of external influences. Where does Jesus tell us this battle originates? (See Matthew 15:18–20.)

    SUGGESTED RESPONSE: *Evil is not a result of what we do or what is around us; it is a result of what is inside us. Evil comes from our sinful hearts.*

6. We can't cure ourselves of double-mindedness. We need the "strong medicine" of Scripture to cleanse and purify our hearts. Read each of the following Scripture passages and write down the remedy for eliminating double-mindedness.

3. What do James 1:5–8 and 4:7–8 reveal about double-mindedness as an obstacle to seeking God's guidance and experiencing spiritual growth?

4. The apostle Paul gives a great explanation of the nature of spiritual double-mindedness in Romans 7:18–24. What does he seem to think is the cause of double-mindedness, and what does he think he can do about it?

5. Some people think the battle of double-mindedness versus single-mindedness is a result of external influences. Where does Jesus tell us this battle originates? (See Matthew 15:18–20.)

6. We can't cure ourselves of double-mindedness. We need the "strong medicine" of Scripture to cleanse and purify our hearts. Read each of the following Scripture passages and write down the remedy for eliminating double-mindedness.

PLANNING NOTES

Scripture	Remedy for curing double-mindedness
Psalm 1:1–3	*The person who delights in the law of the Lord and meditates on it day and night is blessed — strong, healthy, fruitful.*
Psalm 119:9–11	*Purity and single focus come from seeking God with a whole heart, committed obedience to God's Word, and "hiding" or treasuring God's Word in our hearts.*
Romans 12:2	*To not be conformed to the world, we need to be transformed by the renewing of our minds (the re-forming that comes by immersing ourselves in Scripture). Then we will be able to know God's will.*
Ephesians 5:25–26	*Those of us who are Christians — the "bride of Christ" — are made without blemish by the washing with water through the Word. We are to read the Bible and allow it to "wash" our minds. We need God-inspired words to move through the fibers of our lives at the deepest levels, lifting out and removing the impurities of sin.*
Colossians 3:16–17	*We need to allow the Word of Christ to dwell in us "richly" and to do everything in the name of Jesus.*

 7. According to 2 Timothy 3:16–17, what does Scripture accomplish in our lives?

SUGGESTED RESPONSE: *Scripture is "useful" for teaching, reproof, correction, and training. As we read and meditate on Scripture, it focuses our minds and hearts on God. The result is that every follower of Jesus "may be thoroughly equipped for every good work."*

We will now break into groups of three to five to complete the Small Group Exploration, which begins on page 75. I will give you a one-minute notice before we rejoin for our Group Discussion.

Did You Know?

- Biblical meditation can't be done quickly. The Bible compares it to the process by which roots draw moisture to nurture and bring fruitfulness to a great tree.
- Biblical meditation is so important that it's mentioned more than fifty times in the Old Testament!
- Meditation implies sustained attention and is built around a simple principle: "What the mind repeats, it retains."
- The purpose behind biblical meditation is not to receive a high score on "heaven's entrance exam." Rather, it's for us to become transformed into people from whom goodness flows like an unceasing stream of water.

Worry is a form of meditation!

Scripture	Remedy for curing double-mindedness
Psalm 1:1–3	
Psalm 119:9–11	
Romans 12:2	
Ephesians 5:25–26	
Colossians 3:16–17	

PLANNING NOTES

---

7. According to 2 Timothy 3:16–17, what does Scripture accomplish in our lives?

Did You Know?

- Biblical meditation can't be done quickly. The Bible compares it to the process by which roots draw moisture to nurture and bring fruitfulness to a great tree.
- Biblical meditation is so important that it's mentioned more than fifty times in the Old Testament!
- Meditation implies sustained attention and is built around a simple principle: "What the mind repeats, it retains."
- The purpose behind biblical meditation is not to receive a high score on "heaven's entrance exam." Rather, it's for us to become transformed into people from whom goodness flows like an unceasing stream of water.

SMALL GROUP EXPLORATION

God Wants to Guide Us

We need guidance in order to pursue the "one important thing"—God's kingdom and his righteousness—and God provides guidance through the Holy Spirit. If we are to live transformed lives, we must learn to be receptive and responsive to the "leadings" or "promptings" of the Holy Spirit. Let's explore how God chooses to communicate to and guide his people.

1. How do we know God wants to guide us? (See Psalm 25:9; 32:8; Proverbs 3:5–6.)

2. What does God say about listening to him? (See John 10:2–5, 27.)

3. We aren't always receptive to or discerning of God's guidance. Read the following Scripture passages and note what happened when God had something to say. Then consider what you need to learn about listening for God's voice.

   a. Genesis 28:10–22

Small Group Exploration • *10 minutes*

Participant's Guide page 75.

God Wants to Guide Us

We need guidance in order to pursue the "one important thing"—God's kingdom and his righteousness—and God provides guidance through the Holy Spirit. So if we are to live transformed lives, we must learn to be receptive and responsive to the "leadings" or "promptings" of the Holy Spirit. Let's explore how God chooses to communicate to and guide his people.

1. How do we know God wants to guide us? (See Psalm 25:9; 32:8; Proverbs 3:5–6.)

   SUGGESTED RESPONSE: *Scripture clearly says God will guide humble people in doing what is right and will teach them his ways. He will instruct us, counsel us, and watch over us. If we trust God and don't depend on our own understanding, he will direct our paths.*

2. What does God say about listening to him? (See John 10:2–5, 27.)

   SUGGESTED RESPONSE: *God emphasizes how important it is for us to listen to him. Jesus stated that his sheep (those who have received him as Lord and Savior) learn to recognize his voice and obey him.*

3. We aren't always receptive to or discerning of God's guidance. Read the following Scripture passages and note what happened when God had something to say. Then consider what you need to learn about listening for God's voice.

   a. Genesis 28:10–22

   SUGGESTED RESPONSE: *While Jacob was sleeping, God spoke to him in a dream and promised to be with him—to guide and protect him. When Jacob woke up, he was surprised by how unaware of God's presence he had been. He thought,* Surely the LORD is in this place, and I was not aware of it. *He evidently*

SMALL GROUP EXPLORATION

God Wants to Guide Us

We need guidance in order to pursue the "one important thing"—God's kingdom and his righteousness—and God provides guidance through the Holy Spirit. If we are to live transformed lives, we must learn to be receptive and responsive to the "leadings" or "promptings" of the Holy Spirit. Let's explore how God chooses to communicate to and guide his people.

1. How do we know God wants to guide us? (See Psalm 25:9; 32:8; Proverbs 3:5–6.)

2. What does God say about listening to him? (See John 10:2–5, 27.)

3. We aren't always receptive to or discerning of God's guidance. Read the following Scripture passages and note what happened when God had something to say. Then consider what you need to learn about listening for God's voice.

   a. Genesis 28:10–22

PLANNING NOTES

had been operating on spiritual autopilot, so he set up an altar and made a vow to help him remember how close God was to him and how much he needed to follow God.

b. 1 Samuel 3:1–11

SUGGESTED RESPONSE: *God called to young Samuel during the night, but communication from God at that time was rare and Samuel didn't recognize God's voice. The boy ran to Eli, the priest, who told the boy he hadn't called him. Then God called out to Samuel again. Samuel again went to Eli, who told him the same thing. After God called Samuel a third time, Eli told the boy to say, "Speak, LORD, for your servant is listening." Samuel did this and learned to discern when God was speaking to him. This reveals that God can indeed speak to us, but we need to learn to recognize his voice.*

c. Numbers 22:10–13, 18–34

SUGGESTED RESPONSE: *Balaam wasn't getting the message God sent and was blind to the presence of God's angel. So God spoke to Balaam through the mouth of a donkey! God went to such great lengths because Balaam was on a path that God considered to be "reckless." Once God finally got Balaam's attention, Balaam redirected his focus to what God wanted.*

4. Psalm 119:97–104 is a psalm of joy and appreciation for God's Word. Note the ways the psalmist has found God's Word to be a source of guidance.

SUGGESTED RESPONSE: *Meditating on God's Word makes us wise, gives insight and understanding, guides us away from evil, and trains us to hate every wrong path.*

5. God not only speaks to us directly and through his Word, he uses other people to convey his message. Note the different ways God can communicate in each of the following passages.

a. Acts 4:25

SUGGESTED RESPONSE: *The early Christians reaffirmed in their prayer that the Holy Spirit had spoken through the psalmist David.*

b. 1 Samuel 3:1–11

c. Numbers 22:10–13, 18–34

4. Psalm 119:97–104 is a psalm of joy and appreciation for God's Word. Note the ways the psalmist has found God's Word to be a source of guidance.

5. God not only speaks to us directly and through his Word, he uses other people to convey his message. Note the different ways God can communicate in each of the following passages.

a. Acts 4:25

b. John 12:49–50

c. Matthew 10:17–20

PLANNING NOTES

b. John 12:49–50

SUGGESTED RESPONSE: *Jesus said his Father commanded him what to say and how to say it, so that what he spoke was what his Father wanted him to say.*

c. Matthew 10:17–20

SUGGESTED RESPONSE: *Jesus promised his followers that during times of persecution the Holy Spirit would give them the words to say.*

> Let participants know when one minute remains.
>
> When time is up, ask the groups to rejoin as one group.

Group Discussion • 6 minutes

> Participant's Guide page 77.
>
> As time permits, discuss the following questions that will help participants explore their understanding of the concepts covered in this session.

Now it's time for us to wrap up our discovery time. Please turn to page 77.

1. How has what we have explored today influenced your view of what is involved in pursuing God's kingdom?

2. In what specific ways has your appreciation for the importance of biblical meditation changed as a result of this session?

3. Before we explored this session, what did you honestly think was involved in seeking God's guidance? What difference will what we learned today make in how you seek God's guidance in the future?

> As part of your discussion, you may want to refer to the chart "What Guidance Is . . . and Is Not" on page 78 of the Participant's Guide.

b. 1 Samuel 3:1–11

c. Numbers 22:10–13, 18–34

4. Psalm 119:97–104 is a psalm of joy and appreciation for God's Word. Note the ways the psalmist has found God's Word to be a source of guidance.

5. God not only speaks to us directly and through his Word, he uses other people to convey his message. Note the different ways God can communicate in each of the following passages.

a. Acts 4:25

b. John 12:49–50

c. Matthew 10:17–20

PLANNING NOTES

GROUP DISCUSSION

1. How has what we have explored today influenced your view of what is involved in pursuing God's kingdom?

2. In what specific ways has your appreciation for the importance of biblical meditation changed as a result of this session?

3. Before we explored this session, what did you honestly think was involved in seeking God's guidance? What difference will what we learned today make in how you seek God's guidance in the future?

What Guidance Is . . . and Is Not	
Guidance is . . .	**Guidance is not . . .**
Necessary in order to live life as Jesus would live it if he were in our place. We seek guidance for the growth of our souls, so that we can become the people God has called us to be.	Just a source of "insider" information to help us get what we want — money, happiness, success, etc. Nor is it something we seek only when we're in trouble or facing a difficult decision.
Given by God. Although we seek it, it's not something we earn.	A badge of spirituality or importance.
Active, not passive. Seeking guidance includes praying, exercising judgment and wisdom, taking initiative, and making responsible choices.	A way to avoid taking action. Just being passive and doing whatever comes along does not guarantee we are in God's will.
A process involving choices and risks. God uses guidance to help us become the right kind of people.	A way to avoid taking risks, a shortcut to decision making, or a way for God to get us to perform the right actions.

4. In what new ways have you realized that God could communicate his guidance to us?

What Guidance Is . . . and Is Not

Guidance is . . .	Guidance is not . . .
Necessary in order to live life as Jesus would live it if he were in our place. We seek guidance for the growth of our souls, so that we can become the people God has called us to be.	Just a source of "insider" information to help us get what we want — money, happiness, success, etc. Nor is it something we seek only when we're in trouble or facing a difficult decision.
Given by God. Although we seek it, it's not something we earn.	A badge of spirituality or importance.
Active, not passive. Seeking guidance includes praying, exercising judgment and wisdom, taking initiative, and making responsible choices.	A way to avoid taking action. Just being passive and doing whatever comes along does not guarantee we are in God's will.
A process involving choices and risks. God uses guidance to help us become the right kind of people.	A way to avoid taking risks, a shortcut to decision making, or a way for God to get us to perform the right actions.

4. In what new ways have you realized that God could communicate his guidance to us?

PERSONAL JOURNEY: TO DO NOW

(**6 MINUTES**)

> Participant's Guide page 79.

Now let's turn to page 79 and spend a few minutes alone with God to review the key points and begin considering how what we've explored today makes a difference in our daily lives.

1. *God calls us to one thing in life—to pursue God's kingdom and his righteousness above all else.* The problem is, we tend to be double-minded: we want to do one thing but do the opposite; we say we're doing one thing while we're really doing something else. The practice of biblical meditation penetrates, cleanses, and transforms our hearts and minds, teaching us how to live fruitful lives for the kingdom of God. As we immerse ourselves in Scripture, we are transformed from double-mindedness to the single focus of pursuing God's kingdom.

What Guidance Is ... and Is Not

Guidance is ...	Guidance is not ...
Necessary in order to live life as Jesus would live it if he were in our place. We seek guidance for the growth of our souls, so that we can become the people God has called us to be.	Just a source of "insider" information to help us get what we want — money, happiness, success, etc. Nor is it something we seek only when we're in trouble or facing a difficult decision.
Given by God. Although we seek it, it's not something we earn.	A badge of spirituality or importance.
Active, not passive. Seeking guidance includes praying, exercising judgment and wisdom, taking initiative, and making responsible choices.	A way to avoid taking action. Just being passive and doing whatever comes along does not guarantee we are in God's will.
A process involving choices and risks. God uses guidance to help us become the right kind of people.	A way to avoid taking risks, a shortcut to decision making, or a way for God to get us to perform the right actions.

4. In what new ways have you realized that God could communicate his guidance to us?

PERSONAL JOURNEY: TO DO NOW

1. *God calls us to one thing in life—to pursue his kingdom and his righteousness above all else.* The problem is, we tend to be double-minded: we want to do one thing but do the opposite; we say we're doing one thing while we're really doing something else. The practice of biblical meditation penetrates, cleanses, and transforms our hearts and minds, teaching us how to live fruitful lives for the kingdom of God. As we immerse ourselves in Scripture, we are transformed from double-mindedness to the single focus of pursuing God's kingdom.

If you asked your family members and/or close friends to describe you in terms of simplicity of heart and double-mindedness, would they say your life is characterized primarily by the desire to seek the kingdom of God and his righteousness? Or would they say you are pursuing many directions?

Write down the ways *you* would say your life is characterized by double-mindedness or by seeking the kingdom of God above all else.

PLANNING NOTES

If you asked your family members and/or close friends to describe you in terms of simplicity of heart and double-mindedness, would they say your life is characterized primarily by the desire to seek the kingdom of God and his righteousness? Or would they say you are pursuing many directions?

Write down the ways *you* would say your life is characterized by double-mindedness or by seeking the kingdom of God above all else.

2. *We need the Holy Spirit's guidance in order to discover how to live as Jesus would live if he were in our place.* The guidance of the Holy Spirit is not reserved for "important," "spiritually mature," or "more spiritual" people; it is available to each of us. The Holy Spirit can and will provide guidance when we seek the kingdom of God above all else. Learning to be receptive and responsive to the leadings or promptings of the Holy Spirit is nonoptional if we are to live transformed lives.

   Think about a time when God used the Bible or someone else to give you Spirit-guided wisdom. How did you respond then, and how might you respond differently to God's voice now?

   To what extent has God's guidance influenced your life—choices, desires, actions, where you go, who you talk to, where you work?

   In what ways might your daily life change if you listened for the Spirit continually, such as pausing during the day to ask God for wisdom?

3. *Seeking God's guidance is an intentional choice. It is not a passive avoidance of responsibility, a shortcut to making decisions, or a way to escape risk.* Seeking God's guidance involves prayer as well as exercising judgment, wisdom, initiative, choice, and responsibility. To seek God's guidance means learning to listen for the Spirit in all things and to be relentlessly responsive to pursuing God's will. God guides us not so we will perform the right actions but so we will learn how to become the right kind of people, so we will learn how to live in the context of seeking his kingdom.

PERSONAL JOURNEY: TO DO NOW

1. *God calls us to one thing in life—to pursue his kingdom and his righteousness above all else.* The problem is, we tend to be double-minded: we want to do one thing but do the opposite; we say we're doing one thing while we're really doing something else. The practice of biblical meditation penetrates, cleanses, and transforms our hearts and minds, teaching us how to live fruitful lives for the kingdom of God. As we immerse ourselves in Scripture, we are transformed from double-mindedness to the single focus of pursuing God's kingdom.

If you asked your family members and/or close friends to describe you in terms of simplicity of heart and double-mindedness, would they say your life is characterized primarily by the desire to seek the kingdom of God and his righteousness? Or would they say you are pursuing many directions?

Write down the ways *you* would say your life is characterized by double-mindedness or by seeking the kingdom of God above all else.

PLANNING NOTES

2. *We need the Holy Spirit's guidance in order to discover how to live as Jesus would live if he were in our place.* The guidance of the Holy Spirit is not reserved for "important," "spiritually mature," or "more spiritual" people; it is available to each of us. The Holy Spirit can and will provide guidance when we seek the kingdom of God above all else. Learning to be receptive and responsive to the leadings or promptings of the Holy Spirit is nonoptional if we are to live transformed lives.

Think about a time when God used the Bible or someone else to give you Spirit-guided wisdom. How did you respond then, and how might you respond differently to God's voice now?

To what extent has God's guidance influenced your life—choices, desires, actions, where you go, who you talk to, where you work?

In what ways might your daily life change if you listened for the Spirit continually, such as pausing during the day to ask God for wisdom?

3. *Seeking God's guidance is an intentional choice. It is not a passive avoidance of responsibility, a shortcut to making decisions, or a way to escape risk.* Seeking God's guidance involves prayer, exercising judgment, wisdom, initiative, choice, and responsibility. To seek God's guidance means learning to listen for the Spirit in all things and to be relentlessly responsive to pursuing God's will. God guides us not so we will perform the right actions but so we will learn how to become the right kind of people, so we will learn how to live in the context of seeking his kingdom.

In what ways have you sought God's guidance as an attempt to gain "insider" information, or to avoid responsibility or risk? What would be a better motivation for seeking his guidance for those situations?

If you were to actively seek God's guidance on a daily basis, how might that strengthen your relationship with him?

In what ways have you sought God's guidance as an attempt to gain "insider" information, or to avoid responsibility or risk? What would be a better motivation for seeking his guidance for those situations?

If you were to actively seek God's guidance on a daily basis, how might that strengthen your relationship with him?

> Let participants know when there is one minute remaining.
>
> When time is up, remind participants that they may want to continue their journey on their own time by completing the exercise on pages 82–83 of their Participant's Guide. Then end the session with the Closing Meditation.

Personal Journey: To Do on Your Own

There's no better time than right now to begin putting into practice what you've learned today about living an undivided life that is focused on God and his Word. Set aside time within the next few days to do the following:

1. Think about the areas of your life in which you tend to be double-minded and write them down.

2. Prayerfully consider why this is a problem for you and write it down. Are you, for example, fearful, holding on to a secret sin, unwilling to make a particular sacrifice, or focused on things of this world?

3. Then begin digging into what Scripture says about those things. Read not only for information, but meditate on the Scripture and listen for God's wisdom and guidance in those specific areas. If the practice of meditating on Scripture is new for you, the following suggestions will help you get started.

3. *Seeking God's guidance is an intentional choice. It is not a passive avoidance of responsibility, a shortcut to making decisions, or a way to escape risk.* Seeking God's guidance involves prayer, exercising judgment, wisdom, initiative, choice, and responsibility. To seek God's guidance means learning to listen for the Spirit in all things and to be relentlessly responsive to pursuing God's will. God guides us not so we will perform the right actions but so we will learn how to become the right kind of people, so we will learn how to live in the context of seeking his kingdom.

In what ways have you sought God's guidance as an attempt to gain "insider" information, or to avoid responsibility or risk? What would be a better motivation for seeking his guidance for those situations?

If you were to actively seek God's guidance on a daily basis, how might that strengthen your relationship with him?

PLANNING NOTES

PERSONAL JOURNEY:
TO DO ON YOUR OWN

There's no better time than right now to begin putting into practice what you've learned today about living an undivided life that is focused on God and his Word. Set aside time within the next few days to do the following:

1. Think about the areas of your life in which you tend to be double-minded and write them down.

2. Prayerfully consider why this is a problem for you and write it down. Are you, for example, fearful, holding on to a secret sin, unwilling to make a particular sacrifice, or focused on things of this world?

3. Then begin digging into what Scripture says about those things. Read not only for information, but meditate on the Scripture and listen for God's wisdom and guidance in those specific areas. If the practice of meditating on Scripture is new for you, the following suggestions will help you get started.

Suggestions for Meditating on Scripture

1. *Ask God to meet you in Scripture.* Acknowledge that he is present with you. Ask him to begin to wash your thoughts. Anticipate that God will speak to you through his Word. You may be deeply moved in reading or be prompted to take a particular course of action.

2. *Read the Bible in a repentant spirit.* Read it with a vulnerable heart, realizing that reading for transformation is different from reading to find information or to prove a point. Resolve to obey the Scriptures.

3. *Meditate on a fairly brief passage or narrative.* Read Scripture slowly. When certain words or thoughts stand out, let them sink into your heart and allow God to use them to speak to you. If you are reading a story, use your imagination to envision the setting and what was happening. "Success" in meditation is not to get through a quantity of Scripture but to get the Scripture through to you.

4. *Take one thought or verse with you through the day.* Fruitful living comes to the person who meditates on Scripture "day and night" (Psalm 1:1–3). Before you go to sleep at night or as soon as you wake up, choose a single piece of Scripture on which to meditate throughout the day. You'll discover wonderful truths!

5. *Allow this thought to become part of your memory.* Memorizing Scripture is a powerful means of transforming your mind. It's not how many words you memorize that matters; it's what happens to your mind as you immerse it in Scripture.

Suggestions for Meditating on Scripture

1. *Ask God to meet you in Scripture.* Acknowledge that he is present with you. Ask him to begin to wash your thoughts. Anticipate that God will speak to you through his Word. You may be deeply moved in reading or be prompted to take a particular course of action.

2. *Read the Bible in a repentant spirit.* Read it with a vulnerable heart, realizing that reading for transformation is different from reading to find information or to prove a point. Resolve to obey the Scriptures.

3. *Meditate on a fairly brief passage or narrative.* Read Scripture slowly. When certain words or thoughts stand out, let them sink into your heart and let God use them to speak to you. If you are reading a story, use your imagination to envision the setting and what was happening. "Success" in meditation is not to get through a quantity of Scripture but to get the Scripture through to you.

4. *Take one thought or verse with you through the day.* Fruitful living comes to the person who meditates on Scripture "day and night" (Psalm 1:1–3). Before you go to sleep at night or as soon as you wake up, choose a single piece of Scripture on which to meditate throughout the day. You'll discover wonderful truths!

5. *Allow this thought to become part of your memory.* Memorizing Scripture is a powerful means of transforming your mind. It's not how many words you memorize that matters; it's what happens to your mind as you immerse it in Scripture.

CLOSING MEDITATION

1 MINUTE

Dear Lord, we learned a lot today about the importance of practicing biblical meditation and seeking your guidance. Please help us to apply what we have learned in the days and weeks ahead. Open our minds and hearts to listen to what you say through Scripture. We acknowledge our need to be transformed by your Word and to learn how to live in the kingdom of God here and now. Give us a renewed hunger to know your Word and be washed through the Holy Spirit's power. Thank you that you are indeed with us and want to guide us according to your will. Fill our minds with thoughts and feelings of truth, love, joy, and humility. Amen.

Suggestions for Meditating on Scripture

1. *Ask God to meet you in Scripture.* Acknowledge that he is present with you. Ask him to begin to wash your thoughts. Anticipate that God will speak to you through his Word. You may be deeply moved in reading or be prompted to take a particular course of action.

2. *Read the Bible in a repentant spirit.* Read it with a vulnerable heart, realizing that reading for transformation is different from reading to find information or to prove a point. Resolve to obey the Scriptures.

3. *Meditate on a fairly brief passage or narrative.* Read Scripture slowly. When certain words or thoughts stand out, let them sink into your heart and allow God to use them to speak to you. If you are reading a story, use your imagination to envision the setting and what was happening. "Success" in meditation is not to get through a quantity of Scripture but to get the Scripture through to you.

4. *Take one thought or verse with you through the day.* Fruitful living comes to the person who meditates on Scripture "day and night" (Psalm 1:1–3). Before you go to sleep at night or as soon as you wake up, choose a single piece of Scripture on which to meditate throughout the day. You'll discover wonderful truths!

5. *Allow this thought to become part of your memory.* Memorizing Scripture is a powerful means of transforming your mind. It's not how many words you memorize that matters; it's what happens to your mind as you immerse it in Scripture.

PLANNING NOTES

Practicing Servanthood, Finding Freedom

BEFORE YOU LEAD
Synopsis

During this session you'll guide participants in dealing with the oldest sin: pride. In the Garden of Eden, Satan tempted Eve with the promise that she would "be like God." Since that day, every human being has wrestled with pride. We each have tried, in one way or another, to take God's place.

Pride is evident in our preoccupation with our appearance and image. Pride leads us to shun correction and defend ourselves. Pride fuels criticism and judgmentalism. Pride pushes us to impress others with our greatness. Pride moves us to exclude instead of to embrace.

Pride hinders our spiritual growth by squelching love, the essence of spiritual life. It destroys our capacity to love God and to love others. Jesus came to earth as a humble servant not because he wanted to *disguise* who God is but in order to *reveal* who God is. So if we are going to live as Jesus would live if he were in our place, we need to deal with our pride problem.

You'll guide participants in discovering the practice of servanthood, which trains us in humility. Humility is not about convincing ourselves or others that we are something we are not. Humility is about recognizing that the universe doesn't revolve around us. Jesus calls us to serve not just because other people need our service but because of the change that takes place inside us when we serve. The practice of servanthood helps us realize the truth about ourselves and sets us free from the endless contest to see who is the greatest. As it turns out, the life we've always wanted is a life of humility!

You'll also help participants discover how to be set free from "approval addiction," which is the need to impress others and to seek their applause and approval. Many of us confuse our performance in some aspect of life with our worth as a person. As a result, we live in bondage to what other people think of us. We need to learn to rest on God's acceptance rather than the changing opinions of other people. By practicing the discipline of secrecy—doing good things for people but not saying anything about it—we learn to set our hearts in order and let go of the need to congratulate ourselves whenever we succeed.

Key Points of This Session

1. *Pride is the oldest sin, and no matter what form it takes, it is rooted in our attempt to be like God.* Pride has been a persistent problem for the human race since the Garden of Eden. It leads us to be preoccupied with ourselves and to shun correction. It damages our relationships. At its deepest level, pride causes us to exclude God and other people from their rightful place in our hearts. Whereas Jesus said the essence of spiritual life is to love God and to love people, pride destroys our capacity to love.

2. *The practice of servanthood transforms our prideful hearts.* Humility is not about convincing the world that we are something we are not; it is about recognizing the truth that the universe doesn't revolve around us. True servanthood sets us free from the endless contest to see who is the greatest. Jesus calls us to servanthood not just because other people need our service but because of what happens inside us when we serve.

3. *True spiritual maturity sets us free from the bondage of approval addiction. It sets us free from the need to congratulate ourselves when we've gotten something right.* Approval addiction means we are motivated to impress others, to seek their applause and approval. It is the opposite of living as Jesus would live in our place. Acts done to impress others are a form of pride and have no value as spiritual training. But by practicing the discipline of secrecy— doing good things for people but not saying anything about it— we can be released from bondage to approval addiction.

Suggested Reading

Chapters seven and ten of *The Life You've Always Wanted*

SESSION OUTLINE

55 MINUTES

    I. Introduction (5 minutes)
Welcome
What's to Come
Questions to Think About

    II. Video Presentation: "Practicing Servanthood, Finding Freedom" (13 minutes)

    III. Group Discovery (30 minutes)
Video Highlights (5 minutes)
Large Group Exploration (10 minutes)
Small Group Exploration (10 minutes)
Group Discussion (5 minutes)

    IV. Personal Journey (6 minutes)

    V. Closing Meditation (1 minute)

Humility, if we could ever grow into it, would not be a burden. It would be an immense gift. Humility is the freedom to stop trying to be what we're not, or pretending to be what we're not, and accepting our "appropriate smallness." In Luther's words, humility is the decision to "let God be God."

—John Ortberg

Practicing Servanthood, Finding Freedom

(SESSION FIVE)

INTRODUCTION

(5 MINUTES)

Welcome

> Participant's Guide page 85.
>
> Welcome participants to *The Life You've Always Wanted*, session five, "Practicing Servanthood, Finding Freedom."

What's to Come

During this session, we'll discover the spiritual disciplines that train us to deal with pride and what John Ortberg calls "approval addiction" or "impression management." Pride is the oldest sin, and it leads us to be preoccupied with ourselves and to shun correction. It also destroys our capacity to love God and other people. We simply cannot begin to live as Jesus would live if he were in our place if we're caught in the trap of comparing ourselves to others and impressing them in order to gain their approval. So we will learn how practicing the disciplines of servanthood and secrecy (which is saying nothing about the good things we do) can transform our hearts and lives.

Let's begin by considering a few questions related to pride and living for the approval of other people. These questions are on page 86 of your Participant's Guide.

Practicing Servanthood, Finding Freedom

SESSION FIVE

Humility, if we could ever grow into it, would not be a burden. It would be an immense gift. Humility is the freedom to stop trying to be what we're not, or pretending to be what we're not, and accepting our "appropriate smallness." In Luther's words, humility is the decision to "let God be God."

—John Ortberg

85

---

86 • The Life You've Always Wanted Participant's Guide

QUESTIONS TO THINK ABOUT

1. Define pride and identify the ways it reveals itself in our lives.

2. When you hear the word *servanthood*, what comes to mind? What appeals to you? What repels you?

3. How do you feel when you've pleased someone who is important to you? In what ways does that person's approval influence your thinking and/or future behavior?

Questions to Think About

> Participant's Guide page 86.
>
> As time permits, ask participants to respond to two or more of the following questions.

1. Define pride and identify the ways it reveals itself in our lives.

   Responses will vary, but at its heart pride is an attempt to put ourselves in God's rightful place. Pride shows up in all kinds of ways: when we are preoccupied with our appearance or image, think we are always right, reject correction, look down on other people, try to be better than other people, etc. Encourage participants to think not only of the obvious evidences of pride, but the more subtle ones as well. It's important to begin seeing how pervasive pride is in our culture and our personal lives.

2. When you hear the word *servanthood,* what comes to mind? What appeals to you? What repels you?

   Participants are likely to mention a number of images such as: a maid, someone who does chores for people, someone who is not paid much for his or her work, a doormat. They might also describe someone who does good things for other people. Some participants may admire some images of servanthood, such as working behind the scenes without receiving recognition, while others are offended by the lack of recognition. The point here is not only to identify the participants' images of servanthood, but their feelings toward it.

3. How do you feel when you've pleased someone who is important to you? In what ways does that person's approval influence your thinking and/or future behavior?

   Responses will vary, but approval makes us feel good about ourselves. Approval validates our success, and most of us want more and more of it. We may go to great lengths to get people to think or say good things about us and go to equally great lengths to avoid negative feedback. It will be very helpful for participants to consider how what John Ortberg calls "approval addiction"

QUESTIONS TO THINK ABOUT

1. Define pride and identify the ways it reveals itself in our lives.

2. When you hear the word *servanthood,* what comes to mind? What appeals to you? What repels you?

3. How do you feel when you've pleased someone who is important to you? In what ways does that person's approval influence your thinking and/or future behavior?

PLANNING NOTES

influences our daily behavior and causes us to focus our attention on "impression management" rather than on authentic living.

Let's keep these ideas in mind as we view the video. There is space to take notes on page 87 of your Participant's Guide.

VIDEO PRESENTATION:

"PRACTICING SERVANTHOOD, FINDING FREEDOM"

13 MINUTES

Participant's Guide page 87.

Video Observations

The Messiah complex—symptom of pride

The ministries of servanthood

Approval addiction

The discipline of secrecy

VIDEO OBSERVATIONS

The Messiah complex—symptom of pride

The ministries of servanthood

Approval addiction

The discipline of secrecy

PLANNING NOTES

GROUP DISCOVERY

(**30** MINUTES)

> **If your group has seven or more members,** use the Video Highlights with the entire group (5 minutes), then complete the Large Group Exploration (10 minutes), and break into small groups of three to five people for the Small Group Exploration (10 minutes). At the end, bring everyone together for the closing Group Discussion (5 minutes).
>
> **If your group has fewer than seven members,** begin with the Video Highlights (5 minutes), then complete both the Large Group Exploration (10 minutes) and the Small Group Exploration (10 minutes). Wrap up your discovery time with the Group Discussion (5 minutes).

Please turn to page 88 of your Participant's Guide.

Video Highlights • 5 minutes

> Participant's Guide page 88.
>
> As time permits, ask one or more of the following questions, which directly relate to the video the participants have just seen.

1. In what ways has your view of the practice of servanthood changed or been challenged by what you saw in the video?

   SUGGESTED RESPONSE: *Although some participants began this session with a positive view of servanthood, it is likely that many participants have viewed servanthood rather negatively—as something they have an obligation to do in order to be "good Christians." John Ortberg presents servanthood in terms of a practice that accomplishes something good and desirable in us; it sets us free from bondage to pride. Instead of serving as an effort to prove how "humble" we are (when, in fact, we may have little interest in humility) or serving to win the approval of other people, servanthood is the practice by which our hearts are transformed from pride to humility.*

VIDEO HIGHLIGHTS

1. In what ways has your view of the practice of servanthood changed or been challenged by what you saw in the video?

2. John Ortberg mentioned several ministries of daily life—the ministry of the mundane, the ministry of interruptions, the ministry of holding your tongue, and so on. How does viewing these daily occurrences as opportunities to practice servanthood change the way we respond to them?

3. Why do you think the discipline of secrecy is hard to practice?

PLANNING NOTES

2. John Ortberg mentioned several ministries of daily life—the ministry of the mundane, the ministry of interruptions, the ministry of holding your tongue, and so on. In what way(s) does viewing these daily occurrences as opportunities to practice servanthood change the way we respond to them?

   SUGGESTED RESPONSE: *Often we view interruptions and the needs of other people negatively because they get in the way of what we'd rather be doing and seem to lessen our importance. But if we are looking for ways in which God can use us to serve others, these become opportunities to live as Jesus would live. Choosing the path of servanthood trains us in humility, teaching us the essential truth that the universe doesn't revolve around us.*

3. Why do you think the discipline of secrecy is hard to practice?

   SUGGESTED RESPONSE: *Although a few participants may already be practicing this discipline and have discovered how liberating it can be, many of us find it hard to practice the discipline of secrecy. It's hard to do good things and not let other people know about it. We may not like being at the mercy of people's opinions of us, yet we encourage (and even crave) their positive feedback.*

Please turn to page 89 of your Participant's Guide, and let's explore the truth about pride and how to be set free from its bondage.

Large Group Exploration • 10 minutes

Participant's Guide page 89.

The Transforming Power of Servanthood

Pride is a persistent human problem. It is so deeply rooted in us that it is even easy for us to become proud of our spiritual growth! Pride can be so subtle, yet it always leads us to be preoccupied with ourselves and our comparative worth. Whereas Jesus said the essence of spiritual life is to love God and to love people, pride destroys that capacity.

In contrast, the practice of servanthood sets us free from the endless contest to see who is the greatest. It helps us to recognize that the world doesn't revolve around us and in the process trains us in humility. Let's explore the sin of pride and the grace of humility to discover how we can pursue humility in everyday life.

VIDEO HIGHLIGHTS

1. In what ways has your view of the practice of servanthood changed or been challenged by what you saw in the video?

2. John Ortberg mentioned several ministries of daily life—the ministry of the mundane, the ministry of interruptions, the ministry of holding your tongue, and so on. How does viewing these daily occurrences as opportunities to practice servanthood change the way we respond to them?

3. Why do you think the discipline of secrecy is hard to practice?

LARGE GROUP EXPLORATION

The Transforming Power of Servanthood

Pride is a persistent human problem. It is so deeply rooted in us that it is even easy to become proud of our spiritual growth! Pride can be so subtle, yet it always leads us to be preoccupied with ourselves and our comparative worth. Whereas Jesus said the essence of spiritual life is to love God and to love people, pride destroys that capacity.

In contrast, the practice of servanthood sets us free from the endless contest to see who is the greatest. It helps us to recognize that the world doesn't revolve around us and in the process trains us in humility. Let's explore the sin of pride and the grace of humility to discover how we can pursue humility in everyday life.

1. How did the serpent tempt Eve to eat the forbidden fruit in the Garden of Eden? (See Genesis 3:4–5.)

2. What are the consequences of pride in our actions and in our hearts? (See Psalm 10:4; Proverbs 11:2; 13:10; 1 Corinthians 13:4.)

PLANNING NOTES

1. How did the serpent tempt Eve to eat the forbidden fruit in the Garden of Eden? (See Genesis 3:4–5.)

   SUGGESTED RESPONSE: *The serpent appealed to her pride, saying that if she ate the fruit she'd "be like God." This makes pride the oldest sin found in the Bible.*

2. What are the consequences of pride in our actions and in our hearts? (See Psalm 10:4; Proverbs 11:2; 13:10; 1 Corinthians 13:4.)

   SUGGESTED RESPONSE: *Pride leads to all sorts of trouble including disgrace and quarrels. It is opposed to love. But the greatest tragedy is that the proud do not seek God; they have no room for him.*

3. From the beginning to the end of Scripture, God denounces pride again and again. What is God's response to pride as recorded in Leviticus 26:18–19; Proverbs 16:5; Malachi 4:1; and Luke 20:46–47?

   SUGGESTED RESPONSE: *God hates pride and will punish and destroy proud people.*

4. What symptoms of pride are evident in the parable Jesus told in Luke 18:9–14? (See especially verses 9–12.)

   SUGGESTED RESPONSE: *The Pharisee, who thanked God he was not a sinner like robbers, evildoers, adulterers, and the corrupt tax collector who prayed near him, unknowingly revealed the great depth of his own pride. He was self-absorbed and an obvious approval addict. He repeatedly compared himself to other people, was enamored with his self-righteousness, and was critical and judgmental of others. It is unlikely that he would have responded positively to correction. These are the same symptoms of pride evident in us today.*

LARGE GROUP EXPLORATION

The Transforming Power of Servanthood

Pride is a persistent human problem. It is so deeply rooted in us that it is even easy to become proud of our spiritual growth! Pride can be so subtle, yet it always leads us to be preoccupied with ourselves and our comparative worth. Whereas Jesus said the essence of spiritual life is to love God and to love people, pride destroys that capacity.

In contrast, the practice of servanthood sets us free from the endless contest to see who is the greatest. It helps us to recognize that the world doesn't revolve around us and in the process trains us in humility. Let's explore the sin of pride and the grace of humility to discover how we can pursue humility in everyday life.

1. How did the serpent tempt Eve to eat the forbidden fruit in the Garden of Eden? (See Genesis 3:4–5.)

2. What are the consequences of pride in our actions and in our hearts? (See Psalm 10:4; Proverbs 11:2; 13:10; 1 Corinthians 13:4.)

---

3. From the beginning to the end of Scripture, God denounces pride again and again. What is God's response to pride as recorded in the following passages: Leviticus 26:18–19; Proverbs 16:5; Malachi 4:1; and Luke 20:46–47?

4. What symptoms of pride are evident in the parable Jesus told in Luke 18:9–14? (See especially verses 9–12.)

Telltale Signs of Pride

VANITY: Perhaps the most common manifestation of pride, vanity is a preoccupation with our appearance or image.

STUBBORNNESS: This form of pride causes us to shun correction and renders us unable to stop defending ourselves. If someone points out an error or flaw, our response is to evade, deny, or blame.

EXCLUSION: At its deepest level, pride destroys our capacity to love. It leads us to exclude both God and other people from their rightful place in our hearts. We compare ourselves to others and aren't satisfied until we convince ourselves that we are better, smarter, wealthier, etc.

PLANNING NOTES

Telltale Signs of Pride

VANITY: Perhaps the most common manifestation of pride, vanity is a preoccupation with our appearance or image.

STUBBORNNESS: This form of pride causes us to shun correction and renders us unable to stop defending ourselves. If someone points out an error or flaw, our response is to evade, deny, or blame.

EXCLUSION: At its deepest level, pride destroys our capacity to love. It leads us to exclude both God and other people from their rightful place in our hearts. We compare ourselves to others and aren't satisfied until we convince ourselves that we are better, smarter, wealthier, etc.

---

5. In contrast to pride, humility gives us the freedom to stop trying or pretending to be what we're not. It allows us to accept our "appropriate smallness" so we can cease being preoccupied with ourselves and instead focus on and serve other people as Jesus would if he were in our place.

   a. How does the apostle Paul describe the life of humility and servanthood, and who is our example to follow? (See Philippians 2:3–8.)

   SUGGESTED RESPONSE: *Paul describes humility and servanthood as not acting out of our self-serving ambitions but acting out of consideration for the needs of others. He encourages us to have the same attitude, the same motivation, as Jesus had when he took on the nature of a servant in order to reveal who God is. Serving—even to the point of death on a cross—is God's business!*

   b. What did Jesus specifically teach his disciples about servanthood, and who was their example to follow? (See Matthew 20:25–28.)

   SUGGESTED RESPONSE: *When Jesus' disciples were struggling with pride, Jesus explained to them how things worked in his kingdom. He explained that while rulers on earth make a point of their greatness by using their authority, greatness in his kingdom comes through service to others. He used himself as their example, saying that he didn't come to receive honor, recognition, and service. Instead, he came to serve and give his life so that those who believe in him could be forgiven and receive eternal life.*

3. From the beginning to the end of Scripture, God denounces pride again and again. What is God's response to pride as recorded in the following passages: Leviticus 26:18–19; Proverbs 16:5; Malachi 4:1; and Luke 20:46–47?

4. What symptoms of pride are evident in the parable Jesus told in Luke 18:9–14? (See especially verses 9–12.)

Telltale Signs of Pride

VANITY: Perhaps the most common manifestation of pride, vanity is a preoccupation with our appearance or image.

STUBBORNNESS: This form of pride causes us to shun correction and renders us unable to stop defending ourselves. If someone points out an error or flaw, our response is to evade, deny, or blame.

EXCLUSION: At its deepest level, pride destroys our capacity to love. It leads us to exclude both God and other people from their rightful place in our hearts. We compare ourselves to others and aren't satisfied until we convince ourselves that we are better, smarter, wealthier, etc.

---

5. In contrast to pride, humility gives us the freedom to stop trying or pretending to be what we're not. It allows us to accept our "appropriate smallness" so we can cease being preoccupied with ourselves and instead focus on and serve other people as Jesus would if he were in our place.

   a. How does the apostle Paul describe the life of humility and servanthood, and who is our example to follow? (See Philippians 2:3–8.)

   b. What did Jesus specifically teach his disciples about servanthood, and who was their example to follow? (See Matthew 20:25–28.)

6. How does God respond to humility? (See Proverbs 3:34; Isaiah 66:2.)

PLANNING NOTES

6. How does God respond to humility? (See Proverbs 3:34; Isaiah 66:2.)

SUGGESTED RESPONSE: *God notices those who are humble. He gives grace and honors humble people who obey him.*

We will now break into groups of three to five to complete the Small Group Exploration, which begins on page 92. I will give you a one-minute notice before we rejoin for our Group Discussion.

Small Group Exploration • 10 minutes

> Participant's Guide page 92.

A Life of Freedom: The Practice of Secrecy

In his book *Celebration of Discipline*, Richard Foster writes, "The grace of humility is worked into our lives through the Discipline of service.... Nothing *disciplines* the inordinate desires of the flesh like service, and nothing *transforms* the desires of the flesh like serving in hiddenness. The flesh whines against service but screams against hidden service. It strains and pulls for honor and recognition."

Foster clearly recognizes how greatly we struggle with pride and bondage to "approval addiction." He also recognizes how important it is for our hearts to be purified and changed by the practices of servanthood and secrecy. As much as we may be inclined to fight against these disciplines, they truly set us free.

1. Cain suffered the earliest recorded case of "approval addiction." How do we know he suffered from this malady of the heart, and what were the consequences? (See Genesis 4:1–8.)

   SUGGESTED RESPONSE: *God rejected Cain's sacrifice, and that lack of approval angered Cain. Cain felt out-sacrificed by his brother, Abel, and killed him because he was jealous of God's approval of Abel.*

2. The apostle Paul apparently recognized the risks and destructive power of approval addiction. He frequently warned the early church of its dangers.

5. In contrast to pride, humility gives us the freedom to stop trying or pretending to be what we're not. It allows us to accept our "appropriate smallness" so we can cease being preoccupied with ourselves and instead focus on and serve other people as Jesus would if he were in our place.

   a. How does the apostle Paul describe the life of humility and servanthood, and who is our example to follow? (See Philippians 2:3–8.)

   b. What did Jesus specifically teach his disciples about servanthood, and who was their example to follow? (See Matthew 20:25–28.)

6. How does God respond to humility? (See Proverbs 3:34; Isaiah 66:2.)

SMALL GROUP EXPLORATION

A Life of Freedom: The Practice of Secrecy

In his book *Celebration of Discipline,* Richard Foster writes, "The grace of humility is worked into our lives through the Discipline of service.... Nothing *disciplines* the inordinate desires of the flesh like service, and nothing *transforms* the desires of the flesh like serving in hiddenness. The flesh whines against service but screams against hidden service. It strains and pulls for honor and recognition."

Foster clearly recognizes how greatly we struggle with pride and bondage to "approval addiction." He also recognizes how important it is for our hearts to be purified and changed by the practices of servanthood and secrecy. As much as we may be inclined to fight against these disciplines, they truly set us free.

1. Cain suffered the earliest recorded case of "approval addiction." How do we know he suffered from this malady of the heart, and what were the consequences? (See Genesis 4:1–8.)

2. The apostle Paul apparently recognized the risks and destructive power of approval addiction. He frequently warned the early church of its dangers.

PLANNING NOTES

a. What did Paul reveal about himself in 1 Corinthians 4:3–4?

SUGGESTED RESPONSE: *Evidently Paul wasn't an "approval addict." What the Corinthians thought of him mattered to him, but it didn't matter too much. Criticism no longer rocked his boat. His sense of well-being rested not on the acceptance of others, not even on his own assessment, but on acceptance from God, who would judge him and hold him accountable.*

b. What had Paul learned about approval addiction? (See Galatians 1:10.)

SUGGESTED RESPONSE: *Paul stated that he had stopped trying to please people and sought only to please God. Furthermore, he was well aware that he could not serve Christ if pleasing people was important to him.*

3. Which phrase in John 12:42–43 describes the religious leaders of Jesus' day who refused to commit themselves to becoming Jesus' disciples? From what did these leaders suffer?

SUGGESTED RESPONSE: *They "loved praise from men more than praise from God." They suffered from approval addiction. Acceptance in the synagogue was more important to them than following Christ.*

4. What is the source of our self-worth? (See Romans 8:38–39; Galatians 3:26–29.)

SUGGESTED RESPONSE: *As Christians, we belong to God and his kingdom. We are his heirs. God loves us with an everlasting love that cannot be destroyed.*

5. What do 2 Corinthians 5:9–10 and 1 Thessalonians 4:1 reveal about pleasing God?

SUGGESTED RESPONSE: *Our goal is to please Christ and we can actually please him by what we do, say, and think. One day he will judge us accordingly.*

a. What did Paul reveal about himself in 1 Corinthians 4:3–4?

b. What had Paul learned about approval addiction? (See Galatians 1:10.)

3. Which phrase in John 12:42–43 describes the religious leaders of Jesus' day who refused to commit themselves to becoming Jesus' disciples? From what did these leaders suffer?

4. What is the source of our self-worth? (See Romans 8:38–39; Galatians 3:26–29.)

5. What do 2 Corinthians 5:9–10 and 1 Thessalonians 4:1 reveal about pleasing God?

PLANNING NOTES

6. Jesus actually recommended what John Ortberg calls the practice of secrecy, which helps us gain freedom from approval addiction. Read Matthew 6:1–6, 16–18 and note the instruction and examples Jesus used. Also compare the reward he said will come when we follow or reject his instruction.

> Let participants know when one minute remains.
>
> When time is up, ask the groups to rejoin as one group.

Matthew 6	Jesus' instruction	Reward for public display of goodness	Reward for practicing secrecy
Verse 1	Don't do acts of righteousness — what we would call good things — in order to be seen by other people.	What others think of you by seeing your display of goodness is the only reward you have. God won't reward you.	God will reward what he alone can see.
Verses 2–4	Whatever you give, give it in secret.	When you make a display of your giving so others will honor you, you have already received your full reward.	God will reward what he alone can see.
Verses 5–6	Don't pray to impress others; pray in secret.	When you make a public display of your prayers, you have already received your full reward.	God will reward what he alone can see.
Verses 16–18	Don't fast in such a way that everyone knows you are fasting; keep it a secret.	When you make a public display of your fasting, you have already received your full reward.	God will reward what he alone can see.

6. Jesus actually recommended what John Ortberg calls the practice of secrecy, which helps us gain freedom from approval addiction. Read Matthew 6:1–6, 16–18 and note the instruction and examples Jesus used. Also compare the reward he said will come when we follow or reject his instruction.

Matthew 6	Jesus' instruction	Reward for public display of goodness	Reward for practicing secrecy
Verse 1			
Verses 2–4			
Verses 5–6			
Verses 16–18			

PLANNING NOTES

Group Discussion • 5 minutes

> Participant's Guide page 95.
>
> As time permits, discuss the following questions that will help participants explore their understanding of the concepts covered in this session.

Now it's time for us to wrap up our discovery time. Please turn to page 95.

1. In *The Life You've Always Wanted*, John Ortberg wrote, "The primary reason Jesus calls us to servanthood is not just because other people need our service. It is because of what happens to us when we serve." We've spent some time exploring pride and humility, approval addiction, and the practices of servanthood and secrecy. What changes inside us that enables us to live as Jesus would live if he were in our place? In contrast, what happens when we don't serve?

2. We read in John 13:14 that Jesus washed the disciples' feet and wanted that to be an example to his disciples. What things today might be similar examples of daily service we can render to others?

3. We often think we're pretty clever about disguising our pride. What are some of the ways we try to impress people without letting on that we're trying to impress them?

4. Jesus was totally free from the need to create an impression and that enabled him to serve his Father completely and to speak God's truth in love without concern for what might happen to him. What do you think would change in your life if you were free from the burden of "impression management," of trying to get other people to think about you in a certain way?

5. What do you think John Ortberg meant when he wrote, "Acts of servanthood done to impress others lose their intrinsic power to help us enter the life of the kingdom"?

GROUP DISCUSSION

1. In *The Life You've Always Wanted,* John Ortberg wrote, "The primary reason Jesus calls us to servanthood is not just because other people need our service. It is because of what happens to us when we serve." We've spent some time exploring pride and humility, approval addiction, and the practices of servanthood and secrecy. What changes inside us that enables us to live as Jesus would live if he were in our place? In contrast, what happens when we don't serve?

2. We read in John 13:14 that Jesus washed the disciples' feet and wanted that to be an example to his disciples. What things today might be similar examples of daily service we can render to others?

3. We often think we're pretty clever about disguising our pride. What are some of the ways we try to impress people without letting on that we're trying to impress them?

96 • The Life You've Always Wanted Participant's Guide

4. Jesus was totally free from the need to create an impression and that enabled him to serve his Father completely and to speak God's truth in love without concern for what might happen to him. What do you think would change in your life if you were free from the burden of "impression management," of trying to get other people to think about you in a certain way?

5. What do you think John Ortberg meant when he wrote, "Acts of servanthood done to impress others lose their intrinsic power to help us enter the life of the kingdom"?

PLANNING NOTES

PERSONAL JOURNEY: TO DO NOW

6 MINUTES

> Participant's Guide page 97.

Now let's turn to page 97 and each spend a few minutes alone with God to review the key points and begin considering how what we've explored today makes a difference in our daily lives.

1. *Pride is the oldest sin, and no matter what form it takes, it is rooted in our attempt to be like God.* Pride has been a persistent problem for the human race since the Garden of Eden. It leads us to be preoccupied with ourselves and to shun correction. It damages our relationships. At its deepest level, pride causes us to exclude God and other people from their rightful place in our hearts. Whereas Jesus said the essence of spiritual life is to love God and to love people, pride destroys our capacity to love.

   No matter how well hidden they may be, we all have some struggles with pride. Write down at least three areas or instances of pride.

   NOTE: Look especially hard at areas where you are certain you are "right," where relationships are damaged, where you are sensitive to correction (or where people tend to unfairly criticize you!), or where you feel more important than other people.

2. *The practice of servanthood transforms our prideful hearts.* Humility is not about convincing the world that we are something we are not; it is about recognizing the truth that the universe doesn't revolve around us. True servanthood sets us free from the endless contest to see who is the greatest. Jesus calls us to servanthood not just because other people need our service but because of what happens inside us when we serve.

   What role does servanthood play in your life?

   In what ways has serving other people changed you?

PERSONAL JOURNEY: TO DO NOW

1. *Pride is the oldest sin, and no matter what form it takes, it is rooted in our attempt to be like God.* Pride has been a persistent problem for the human race since the Garden of Eden. It leads us to be preoccupied with ourselves and to shun correction. It damages our relationships. At its deepest level, pride causes us to exclude God and other people from their rightful place in our hearts. Whereas Jesus said the essence of spiritual life is to love God and to love people, pride destroys our capacity to love.

No matter how well hidden they may be, we all have some struggles with pride. Write down at least three areas or instances of pride.

NOTE: Look especially hard at areas where you are certain you are "right," where relationships are damaged, where you are sensitive to correction (or where people tend to unfairly criticize you!), or where you feel more important than other people.

2. *The practice of servanthood transforms our prideful hearts.* Humility is not about convincing the world that we are something we are not; it is about recognizing the truth that the universe doesn't revolve around us. True servanthood sets us free from the endless contest to see who is the greatest. Jesus calls us to servanthood not just because other people need our service but because of what happens inside us when we serve.

What role does servanthood play in your life?

In what ways has serving other people changed you?

If your life is lacking in service, write down some ways you could begin serving other people and set a date to begin doing them.

PLANNING NOTES

If your life is lacking in service, write down some ways you could begin serving other people and set a date to begin doing them.

3. *True spiritual maturity sets us free from the bondage of approval addiction. It sets us free from the need to congratulate ourselves when we've gotten something right.* Approval addiction means we are motivated to impress others, to seek their applause and approval. It is the opposite of living as Jesus would live in our place. Acts done to impress others are a form of pride and have no value as spiritual training. But by practicing the discipline of secrecy—doing good things for people but not saying anything about it—we can be released from bondage to approval addiction.

Think about the people by whose judgment you measure your success or failure: parent(s), teachers, neighbors, coworkers, boss, members of your peer group, etc. How much influence do they *really* wield over you?

Think about the people in your circle of influence. What opportunities do you have to practice doing "secret" things for them? (Give them a gift anonymously? Pray for them? Do a chore for them?)

> Let participants know when there is one minute remaining.
>
> When time is up, remind participants that they may want to continue their journey on their own time by completing the Personal Journey exercises on pages 100–102 of their Participant's Guide. Then end the session with the Closing Meditation.

2. *The practice of servanthood transforms our prideful hearts.* Humility is not about convincing the world that we are something we are not; it is about recognizing the truth that the universe doesn't revolve around us. True servanthood sets us free from the endless contest to see who is the greatest. Jesus calls us to servanthood not just because other people need our service but because of what happens inside us when we serve.

What role does servanthood play in your life?

In what ways has serving other people changed you?

If your life is lacking in service, write down some ways you could begin serving other people and set a date to begin doing them.

PLANNING NOTES

3. *True spiritual maturity sets us free from the bondage of approval addiction. It sets us free from the need to congratulate ourselves when we've gotten something right.* Approval addiction means we are motivated to impress others, to seek their applause and approval. It is the opposite of living as Jesus would live in our place. Acts done to impress others are a form of pride and have no value as spiritual training. But by practicing the discipline of secrecy—doing good things for people but not saying anything about it—we can be released from bondage to approval addiction.

Think about the people by whose judgment you measure your success or failure: parent(s), teachers, neighbors, coworkers, boss, members of your peer group, etc. How much influence do they *really* wield over you?

Think about the people in your circle of influence. What opportunities do you have to practice doing "secret" things for them? (Give them a gift anonymously? Pray for them? Do a chore for them?)

PERSONAL JOURNEY: TO DO ON YOUR OWN

Take time after this session ends to think about what you discovered today. Set aside some time to do the following, which will help you to apply what you learned.

1. Read "Ways We Can Enter a Life of Servanthood" and write down concrete ways in which you can begin implementing these practices in your daily life.

Ways We Can Enter a Life of Servanthood

Choosing to serve others is an antidote to pride. Following are some practical ways in which you can begin entering a life of service today.

Ministries of servanthood	Practical ideas	My ideas
Choose to be involved in the ministry of the mundane.	Help a colleague at work or help take care of a sick child in the middle of the night so your spouse can sleep. When you serve well, cheerfully, and out of the limelight, you may one day start doing it for the joy of it and begin to understand how life in God's kingdom works.	
Choose to be involved in the ministry of availability.	Be willing to be interrupted, to help other people do what isn't on your schedule. Set aside time so you are available to serve others without an agenda of your own. Ask God for wisdom to know when to be available.	

PERSONAL JOURNEY: TO DO ON YOUR OWN

Take time after this session ends to think about what you discovered today. Set aside some time to do the following, which will help you to apply what you learned.

1. Read "Ways We Can Enter a Life of Servanthood" and write down concrete ways in which you can begin implementing these practices in your daily life.

Ways We Can Enter a Life of Servanthood

Choosing to serve others is an antidote to pride. Following are some practical ways in which you can begin entering a life of service today.

Ministries of servanthood	Practical ideas	My ideas
Choose to be involved in the ministry of the mundane.	Help a colleague at work or help take care of a sick child in the middle of the night so your spouse can sleep. When you serve well, cheerfully, and out of the limelight, you may one day start doing it for the joy of it and begin to understand how life in God's kingdom works.	
Choose to be involved in the ministry of availability.	Be willing to be interrupted, to help other people do what isn't on your schedule. Set aside time so you are available to serve others without an agenda of your own. Ask God for wisdom to know when to be available.	
Choose to be involved in the ministry of holding your tongue.	Instead of demonstrating how much you know or how important you are, choose to say nothing. The fate of the world doesn't rest on you or your accomplishments.	
Choose to be involved in the ministry of bearing one another's burdens.	This may mean praying for someone, offering assistance or a comforting word. It may also mean "bearing with" a difficult person until you learn to love him or her or learn to hear God speak through that person.	

PERSONAL JOURNEY: TO DO ON YOUR OWN

Take time after this session ends to think about what you discovered today. Set aside some time to do the following, which will help you to apply what you learned.

1. Read "Ways We Can Enter a Life of Servanthood" and write down concrete ways in which you can begin implementing these practices in your daily life.

Ways We Can Enter a Life of Servanthood

Choosing to serve others is an antidote to pride. Following are some practical ways in which you can begin entering a life of service today.

Ministries of servanthood	Practical ideas	My ideas
Choose to be involved in the ministry of the mundane.	Help a colleague at work or help take care of a sick child in the middle of the night so your spouse can sleep. When you serve well, cheerfully, and out of the limelight, you may one day start doing it for the joy of it and begin to understand how life in God's kingdom works.	
Choose to be involved in the ministry of availability.	Be willing to be interrupted, to help other people do what isn't on your schedule. Set aside time so you are available to serve others without an agenda of your own. Ask God for wisdom to know when to be available.	

Choose to be involved in the ministry of holding your tongue.	Instead of demonstrating how much you know or how important you are, choose to say nothing. The fate of the world doesn't rest on you or your accomplishments.	
Choose to be involved in the ministry of bearing one another's burdens.	This may mean praying for someone, offering assistance or a comforting word. It may also mean "bearing with" a difficult person until you learn to love him or her or learn to hear God speak through that person.	

2. Carefully read through "Symptoms of Approval Addiction" and check any symptoms that describe you. Then write down what you intend to do about each problem area.

✓	Symptoms of approval addiction	What I intend to do
	I am often hurt when other people express less than glowing opinions about me.	
	I habitually compare myself to other people.	
	I am competitive in most ordinary situations.	
	I have a nagging sense I'm not important enough or special enough.	
	I envy someone else's success.	

PLANNING NOTES

2. Carefully read through the "Symptoms of Approval Addiction" and check any symptoms that describe you. Then write down what you intend to do about each problem area.

✓	Symptoms of approval addiction	What I intend to do
	I am often hurt when other people express less than glowing opinions about me.	
	I habitually compare myself to other people.	
	I am competitive in most ordinary situations.	
	I have a nagging sense I'm not important enough or special enough.	
	I envy someone else's success.	
	I try to impress important people.	
	I'm afraid someone will find out how much I worry about receiving approval.	
	My sense of self-esteem depends on whether someone notices how smart, attractive, successful, or _____ I am.	
	I find it difficult to love someone who expresses disapproval of me.	
	The opinions of others really affect me.	
	I measure my accomplishments against those of other people.	
	My concern for what others think inevitably leads me to shade the truth.	
	I resent the person whose approval I seek because too much of my well-being rests in his or her hands.	
	I am consumed by impression management. Much of what I say is to control how other people think of me.	

3. Begin doing "secret" acts of kindness for people in your circle of influence, starting today.

Choose to be involved in the ministry of holding your tongue.	Instead of demonstrating how much you know or how important you are, choose to say nothing. The fate of the world doesn't rest on you or your accomplishments.	
Choose to be involved in the ministry of bearing one another's burdens.	This may mean praying for someone, offering assistance or a comforting word. It may also mean "bearing with" a difficult person until you learn to love him or her or learn to hear God speak through that person.	

2. Carefully read through "Symptoms of Approval Addiction" and check any symptoms that describe you. Then write down what you intend to do about each problem area.

✓	Symptoms of approval addiction	What I intend to do
	I am often hurt when other people express less than glowing opinions about me.	
	I habitually compare myself to other people.	
	I am competitive in most ordinary situations.	
	I have a nagging sense I'm not important enough or special enough.	
	I envy someone else's success.	

I try to impress important people.	
I'm afraid someone will find out how much I worry about receiving approval.	
My sense of self-esteem depends on whether someone notices how smart, attractive, successful, or _____ I am.	
I find it difficult to love someone who expresses disapproval of me.	
The opinions of others really affect me.	
I measure my accomplishments against those of other people.	
My concern for what others think inevitably leads me to shade the truth.	
I resent the person whose approval I seek because too much of my well-being rests in his or her hands.	
I am consumed by impression management. Much of what I say is to control how other people think of me.	

3. Begin doing "secret" acts of kindness for people in your circle of influence, starting today.

Closing Meditation

(**1** minute)

Dear God, it's so easy for us to become proud and judgmental, even when nobody else knows. Thank you for the power you give us and for teaching us the value of servanthood. You also know the battles we fight against approval addiction and how impossible they are to win without your help. Make us willing to practice secrecy so, in your strength, we can receive the freedom we have in Christ. We praise you for your love, and for the fact that you—our mighty God—are pleased by what we do in secret! Amen.

Going the Distance with a Well-Ordered Heart

BEFORE YOU LEAD
Synopsis

In this final session, John Ortberg reminds us that spiritual disciplines lead to freedom—the freedom to be the kind of people God wants us to be and to live the kind of life we've always wanted to live. But pursuing God and his kingdom may yield a life that is quite different from what we expect it to be. Here's why.

Our culture values what we like to call a balanced life, which tends to mean a life that is manageable and relatively pleasant. But God never says his ultimate goal is for us to lead a balanced life. The apostle Paul, for example, vigorously pursued the life of God's kingdom and delighted in it. But his experiences of shipwreck, imprisonment, hunger, beatings, and constant danger hardly match our picture of a balanced life! Yet God allows change, suffering, and hardship in our lives because he wants to cultivate in us something far greater than balance; he wants to cultivate a well-ordered heart.

A well-ordered heart is a heart that follows Jesus and seeks to do what he would do if he were in our place. A well-ordered heart causes us to love what is most worth loving, to love the right thing to the right degree in the right way with the right kind of love. A well-ordered heart is a heart that has been transformed by the practice Paul describes in Colossians 3:17: "And whatever you do, whether in word or deed, do it all in the name of the Lord Jesus." During this session, you'll guide participants in reflecting on how to apply this verse in daily life—doing everything in Jesus' name, in partnership with him, the way he'd do it.

A well-ordered heart is also formed by faithful endurance in the midst of suffering. Obviously we would prefer a life without suffering, but God uses suffering to contribute to our spiritual growth. In James 1:2–4, we read that trials (the testing of our faith) develop perseverance, which in turn produces character and makes our faith mature and complete. During such trials our true values, commitments, and beliefs are revealed. God's testing is an act of love in that it refines, strengthens, and perfects our faith and teaches us spiritual endurance. Without suffering, our spiritual transformation is incomplete.

When we suffer, we always have the option of becoming bitter, defeated, and/or discouraged. But when we endure through faith, seeking to know God and to walk through our suffering in partnership with him, we discover a life of freedom, hope, and love we could not even imagine existed. In the video for this session, John Ortberg describes Mabel, an elderly, blind, deaf, disfigured, and bedridden woman who knew and reflected Jesus in the midst of her suffering. Although her physical life lacked so much of what we think is necessary for a "good" life, her life was full and blessed because she thought about Jesus all the time.

At our core, we want the kind of life Mabel lived—a life filled with joy, gratitude, and simple thankfulness for the gift of living in the awareness of God's closeness. Just as Mabel "morphed," we can morph too, and discover the life we've always wanted.

Key Points of This Session

1. *Many of us desire a perfectly balanced, manageable life, but God wants us to pursue a much higher goal.* God wants to craft in each of us a well-ordered heart. A well-ordered heart seeks to follow Jesus and do what he would do. It loves the right thing to the right degree in the right way with the right kind of love. The pursuit of a well-ordered heart is worthy of our devotion, is achievable even in the most desperate situations, and produces good far beyond our sphere of influence.

2. *A well-ordered heart is a transformed heart.* If our ordinary, fallen hearts are to be transformed into hearts that love the right thing in the right way to the right degree with the right kind of love, we need a plan of action. That heart-changing plan of action consists of focusing the events of our daily lives around knowing Jesus and learning how to be more like him. It can be summarized by Paul's admonition in Colossians 3:17 to do everything in the name of Jesus.

3. *A well-ordered heart is perfected by faithful endurance through suffering.* God allows hardship and suffering in our lives to test our faith—to reveal our true values, commitments, and beliefs. God's testing is an act of love in that it refines, strengthens, and perfects our faith. Our perseverance through suffering produces character and makes our faith mature and complete so we can finish the race of life well. When we endure through faith, seeking to know God and to walk through our suffering in partnership with him, we discover a life of freedom, hope, and love—the life we've always wanted!

Suggested Reading

Chapters twelve and thirteen of *The Life You've Always Wanted*

SESSION OUTLINE

55 MINUTES

     I. Introduction (5 minutes)
Welcome
What's to Come
Questions to Think About

    II. Video Presentation: "Going the Distance with a Well-Ordered Heart"
(14 minutes)

    III. Group Discovery (30 minutes)
Video Highlights (6 minutes)
Large Group Exploration (9 minutes)
Small Group Exploration (9 minutes)
Group Discussion (6 minutes)

    IV. Personal Journey (5 minutes)

    V. Closing Meditation (1 minute)

Above all else, guard your heart, for it is the wellspring of life.

—Proverbs 4:23

Going the Distance with a Well-Ordered Heart

INTRODUCTION

5 MINUTES

Welcome

> Participant's Guide page 103.
>
> Welcome participants to *The Life You've Always Wanted*, session six, "Going the Distance with a Well-Ordered Heart."

What's to Come

Today, in the final session of this series, we're going to consider the value of having a well-ordered heart. We'll look at how our ordinary, fallen hearts are transformed by the practice of focusing on knowing Jesus and doing everything in his name. And we'll see how God uses hardship and suffering to refine, strengthen, and perfect our faith so that we will live a life of freedom, hope, and love—the life we've always wanted.

Let's begin by considering a few questions related to the type of life that is so appealing to us and how we respond to God during difficult times. These questions are on page 104 of your Participant's Guide.

Going the Distance with a Well-Ordered Heart

SESSION SIX

Above all else, guard your heart, for it is the wellspring of life.

Proverbs 4:23

103

QUESTIONS TO THINK ABOUT

1. How often have you thought or said, "I need to get my schedule under control"? Why is this so important to us?

   a. What would a more balanced life look like if you had one?

   b. Do you think God wants you to have a balanced life? Why or why not?

2. Identify times of spiritual growth in your life. What were the dominant circumstances in your life during those times? What role (if any) do you think those circumstances played in that growth?

3. What has kept you going when you have had to walk through dark, painful times or times when you didn't know how things would work out?

PLANNING NOTES

Questions to Think About

> Participant's Guide page 104.
>
> As time permits, ask participants to respond to two or more of the following questions.

1. How often have you thought or said, "I've got to get my schedule under control"? Why is this so important to us?

   Who hasn't thought this at least once? Many of us feel as if our lives are out of control, out of balance, all the time. See how balanced or out-of-balance your group feels and why.

   a. What would a more balanced life look like if you had one?

      Responses will vary, but encourage participants to actually describe their picture of a balanced life. What things would they do or not do? Encourage them to describe a balanced day from morning to night. It is essential to have this image in mind in order to answer the next question.

   b. Do you think God wants you to have a balanced life? Why or why not?

      Most participants will not have considered this question before. We tend to operate on the assumption that God would want this for us, but few of us have evaluated the validity of our assumption. Responses will vary. See if anyone in your group recognizes that God may want us to pursue a more compelling goal—giving our lives to something that is much bigger than ourselves. See if anyone questions the assumption that our lives are supposed to be manageable, convenient, and pleasant. See if anyone sees a possible conflict between pursuing God's kingdom above all else and living a balanced, manageable, convenient life.

2. Identify times of spiritual growth in your life. What were the dominant circumstances in your life during those times? What role (if any) do you think those circumstances played in that growth?

   Answers will vary, but it is likely that participants will mention growth coming during times of suffering, pain, or hardship. See

104 • The Life You've Always Wanted Participant's Guide

QUESTIONS TO THINK ABOUT

1. How often have you thought or said, "I need to get my schedule under control"? Why is this so important to us?

   a. What would a more balanced life look like if you had one?

   b. Do you think God wants you to have a balanced life? Why or why not?

2. Identify times of spiritual growth in your life. What were the dominant circumstances in your life during those times? What role (if any) do you think those circumstances played in that growth?

3. What has kept you going when you have had to walk through dark, painful times or times when you didn't know how things would work out?

PLANNING NOTES

Prayers

Unspoken request

Shae graduation

Kevin Horseman + family

Families in church

Grandma Flanagan

Teresa

Travel mercies

Mary Hicks

if participants make a connection between their response to the circumstances they faced and spiritual growth.

3. What has kept you going when you have had to walk through dark, painful times or times when you didn't know how things would work out?

    SUGGESTED RESPONSE: *Responses of course will vary. What is important to bring out is that all of us face times when we have to walk in darkness and don't know how things will turn out. During those times we have to persevere. Obedience, faith, trust, and our relationship with God tend to become very important during those times.*

    Let's keep these ideas in mind as we view the video. There is space to take notes on page 105 of your Participant's Guide.

VIDEO PRESENTATION:

"GOING THE DISTANCE WITH A WELL-ORDERED HEART"

14 MINUTES

Participant's Guide page 105.

Video Observations

The illusion of a balanced life

Cultivating a well-ordered heart

The value of suffering with God

Mabel—a person who morphed

Writing our lives together with God

104 • The Life You've Always Wanted Participant's Guide

QUESTIONS TO THINK ABOUT

1. How often have you thought or said, "I need to get my schedule under control"? Why is this so important to us?

   a. What would a more balanced life look like if you had one?

   b. Do you think God wants you to have a balanced life? Why or why not?

2. Identify times of spiritual growth in your life. What were the dominant circumstances in your life during those times? What role (if any) do you think those circumstances played in that growth?

3. What has kept you going when you have had to walk through dark, painful times or times when you didn't know how things would work out?

Session Six: Going the Distance with a Well-Ordered Heart • 105

VIDEO OBSERVATIONS

The illusion of a balanced life

Cultivating a well-ordered heart

The value of suffering with God

Mabel—a person who morphed

Writing our lives together with God

PLANNING NOTES

GROUP DISCOVERY

30 MINUTES

> **If your group has seven or more members,** use the Video Highlights with the entire group (6 minutes), then complete the Large Group Exploration (9 minutes), and break into small groups of three to five people for the Small Group Exploration (9 minutes). At the end, bring everyone together for the closing Group Discussion (6 minutes).
>
> **If your group has fewer than seven members,** begin with the Video Highlights (6 minutes), then complete both the Large Group Exploration (9 minutes) and the Small Group Exploration (9 minutes). Wrap up your discovery time with the Group Discussion (6 minutes).

Please turn to page 106 of your Participant's Guide.

Video Highlights • 6 minutes

> Participant's Guide page 106.
>
> As time permits, ask one or more of the following questions, which directly relate to the video the participants have just seen.

1. What surprised you about John Ortberg's perspective on a balanced life?

   SUGGESTED RESPONSE: *This perspective will be new to some participants. Encourage participants to discuss Ortberg's point that God calls us to live a life of faith and obedience and that pursuing such a life requires a much larger goal than balance. It's important for participants to realize that pursuing God's kingdom may lead to hardship rather than pleasure and ease.*

2. How does John Ortberg define a well-ordered heart, and how does it relate to the transformed life we've been exploring in this series?

   SUGGESTED RESPONSE: *A well-ordered heart loves the right thing to the right degree in the right way with the right kind of love. Living a transformed life involves learning to do what Jesus*

Session Six: Going the Distance with a Well-Ordered Heart • 211

VIDEO HIGHLIGHTS

1. What surprised you about John Ortberg's perspective on a balanced life?

2. How does John Ortberg define a well-ordered heart, and how does it relate to the transformed life we've been exploring in this series?

3. When you hear a story like Mabel's, what speaks to you? What would you like to have in common with her life?

4. How do you feel about writing your story with God? What encourages you? What excites you? What scares you?

PLANNING NOTES

would do if he were in our place. Jesus had a perfectly ordered heart, so the two go hand in hand. A well-ordered heart is necessary in order to do what Jesus would do, and when we do what Jesus would do, we love the right thing to the right degree in the right way with the right kind of love.

3. When you hear a story like Mabel's, what speaks to you? What would you like to have in common with her life?

    SUGGESTED RESPONSE: *There is no "correct" answer for this question. Most participants will be humbled, inspired, or amazed by her story. It is important that participants take the next step and begin thinking about what she has that they would like to have and what it may require to obtain it. Obviously we would not welcome the suffering she has had to bear, but if her life is a product of suffering, might it be worth the price? That is the question!*

4. How do you feel about writing your story with God? What encourages you? What excites you? What scares you?

    SUGGESTED RESPONSE: *Again, there is no "correct" answer for this question. The objective is to help participants imagine themselves being a part of what they have been seeing in the video. They, too, have the opportunity to write their story with God.*

Please turn to page 107 of your Participant's Guide and we will explore the value of suffering and how God uses it to promote our spiritual growth.

Large Group Exploration • *9 minutes*

> Participant's Guide page 107.

Perseverance Through Suffering

Perseverance is formed by faithful endurance in the midst of hardship. It is the capacity to press on through hardship and finish well. Any truly meaningful human endeavor requires perseverance, and spiritual transformation is no exception. God allows hardship and suffering in the lives of his people to reveal our true values, commitments, and beliefs. Our perseverance through suffering produces

VIDEO HIGHLIGHTS

1. What surprised you about John Ortberg's perspective on a balanced life?

2. How does John Ortberg define a well-ordered heart, and how does it relate to the transformed life we've been exploring in this series?

3. When you hear a story like Mabel's, what speaks to you? What would you like to have in common with her life?

4. How do you feel about writing your story with God? What encourages you? What excites you? What scares you?

LARGE GROUP EXPLORATION

Perseverance Through Suffering

Perseverance is formed by faithful endurance in the midst of hardship. It is the capacity to press on through hardship and finish well. Any truly meaningful human endeavor requires perseverance, and spiritual transformation is no exception. God allows hardship and suffering in the lives of his people to reveal our true values, commitments, and beliefs. Our perseverance through suffering produces character and makes our faith strong, mature, and complete so we can finish the race of life well.

1. The New Testament writers were convinced that faithful endurance amidst hardship was necessary for spiritual maturity. Let's look at a few passages that reveal their perspectives.

   a. What did James write about how suffering benefits us and how to respond to it? (See James 1:2–4.)

   b. What do Hebrews 12:7 and 12:11 teach us about the purpose and work of suffering?

PLANNING NOTES

character and makes our faith strong, mature, and complete so we can finish the race of life well.

1. The New Testament writers were convinced that faithful endurance amidst hardship was necessary for spiritual maturity. Let's look at a few passages that reveal their perspectives.

    a. What did James write about how suffering benefits us and how to respond to it? (See James 1:2–4.)

        SUGGESTED RESPONSES: *Suffering is something we need because without perseverance, which comes as a result of faithful endurance, we cannot become mature and complete in our faith. So James encourages us to welcome our trials with joy because of the good they accomplish in us.*

        NOTE: *Suffering alone does not guarantee perseverance because we can let it lead to bitterness and discouragement. Only suffering that is endured in faith with perseverance will produce spiritual character.*

    b. What do Hebrews 12:7 and 12:11 teach us about the purpose and work of suffering?

        SUGGESTED RESPONSE: *Hardship is a form of discipline from God. The discipline of hardship is painful, but in those who submit to its training it produces peace and righteousness.*

    c. According to Hebrews 12:1–3, what does our focus need to be if we are to persevere through suffering? What difference does that focus make?

        SUGGESTED RESPONSE: *We need to remember that many people (the "cloud of witnesses") have endured suffering before us. God wants us to keep running the spiritual race before us. Most important, we need to focus on Jesus, who also endured suffering and did so with joy. Keeping our focus on Jesus helps us to finish well, to "not grow weary and lose heart."*

    d. According to Hebrews 11:24–27, Moses is considered one who persevered through trial. How did he do this?

        SUGGESTED RESPONSE: *Moses endured and did not fear because he saw "him who is invisible," meaning Jesus.*

When Peter tried to walk out on the water he took his eyes off of Jesus.

LARGE GROUP EXPLORATION

Perseverance Through Suffering

Perseverance is formed by faithful endurance in the midst of hardship. It is the capacity to press on through hardship and finish well. Any truly meaningful human endeavor requires perseverance, and spiritual transformation is no exception. God allows hardship and suffering in the lives of his people to reveal our true values, commitments, and beliefs. Our perseverance through suffering produces character and makes our faith strong, mature, and complete so we can finish the race of life well.

1. The New Testament writers were convinced that faithful endurance amidst hardship was necessary for spiritual maturity. Let's look at a few passages that reveal their perspectives.

   a. What did James write about how suffering benefits us and how to respond to it? (See James 1:2–4.)

   b. What do Hebrews 12:7 and 12:11 teach us about the purpose and work of suffering?

   c. According to Hebrews 12:1–3, what does our focus need to be if we are to persevere through suffering? What difference does that focus make?

   d. According to Hebrews 11:24–27, Moses is considered one who persevered through trial. How did he do this?

2. Throughout Scripture, Abraham is mentioned as a man of great faith. We see evidence of his courageous and bold faith from the very beginning of his walk with God. But even *his* faith was tested. As he faithfully endured, his faith was refined, strengthened, and perfected. Although his faith was tested a number of times, Abraham's greatest test came when God asked him to sacrifice his son, Isaac—the long-awaited fulfillment of God's promise to him—on Mount Moriah. Let's see what we can learn from his experience. (See Genesis 22:1–12.)

   a. How did Abraham respond to God's request (verses 1–3)?

PLANNING NOTES

2. Throughout Scripture, Abraham is mentioned as a man of great faith. We see evidence of his courageous and bold faith from the very beginning of his walk with God. But even *his* faith was tested. As he faithfully endured, his faith was refined, strengthened, and perfected. Although his faith was tested a number of times, Abraham's greatest test came when God asked him to sacrifice his son, Isaac—the long-awaited fulfillment of God's promise to him—on Mount Moriah. Let's see what we can learn from his experience. (See Genesis 22:1–12.)

   a. How did Abraham respond to God's request (verses 1–3)?

      SUGGESTED RESPONSE: *Abraham did not waver or delay; he obeyed immediately. He left early the next morning. He cut the wood he needed for the sacrifice. He went in the direction God had told him to go.*

   b. How long did it take Abraham to get to the place God had told him to go (verse 4)? What does this reveal about his commitment to obedience? What do you think Abraham might have felt or struggled with during the journey?

      SUGGESTED RESPONSE: *It took three days to arrive in the region of Mount Moriah. This journey reflects the depth of Abraham's commitment to obedience. This was not an impulsive, "I'll do it until it gets difficult" kind of obedience. Abraham had plenty of time to change his mind, to wonder why God seemed to be contradicting his promise. It is likely he experienced some terribly dark and lonely moments during that journey.*

   c. What evidence do you see that Abraham tenaciously held on to the hope that God would be faithful even though the situation looked hopeless (verses 5–9)?

      SUGGESTED RESPONSE: *Abraham told his servants that he and Isaac would return. He told Isaac that God would provide the sacrifice. He built and prepared the altar for a sacrifice.*

   d. When the moment of truth came, Abraham was willing to do what God had called him to do (verses 10–12). What would have to take place in your heart, in your relationship with God, for you to come to that place?

      SUGGESTED RESPONSE: *Abraham persevered even though from a human perspective the situation seemed hopeless. Today*

c. According to Hebrews 12:1–3, what does our focus need to be if we are to persevere through suffering? What difference does that focus make?

d. According to Hebrews 11:24–27, Moses is considered one who persevered through trial. How did he do this?

2. Throughout Scripture, Abraham is mentioned as a man of great faith. We see evidence of his courageous and bold faith from the very beginning of his walk with God. But even *his* faith was tested. As he faithfully endured, his faith was refined, strengthened, and perfected. Although his faith was tested a number of times, Abraham's greatest test came when God asked him to sacrifice his son, Isaac—the long-awaited fulfillment of God's promise to him—on Mount Moriah. Let's see what we can learn from his experience. (See Genesis 22:1–12.)

a. How did Abraham respond to God's request (verses 1–3)?

b. How long did it take Abraham to get to the place God had told him to go (verse 4)? What does this reveal about his commitment to obedience? What do you think Abraham might have felt or struggled with during the journey?

c. What evidence do you see that Abraham tenaciously held on to the hope that God would be faithful even though the situation looked hopeless (verses 5–9)?

d. When the moment of truth came, Abraham was willing to do what God had called him to do (verses 10–12). What would have to take place in your heart, in your relationship with God, for you to come to that place?

PLANNING NOTES

God still calls us to keep walking in faith even when things seem impossible. In order for us to make such a complete commitment, we need to be transformed people. We need to be people in whom God has crafted a well-ordered heart. We need to be people who have learned to live life in partnership with God.

We will now break into groups of three to five to complete the Small Group Exploration, which begins on page 110. I will give you a one-minute notice before we rejoin for our Group Discussion.

Small Group Exploration • *9 minutes*

> Participant's Guide page 110.

The Quest for a Well-Ordered Heart

In Arthurian legend, people devoted themselves to the great quest for the Holy Grail, the ultimate symbol of communion with Christ. Today, the great quest of many people is for a "balanced lifestyle." But in God's kingdom, there is only one goal truly worthy of human devotion: pursuing a well-ordered heart. The transformation of our ordinary, fallen hearts into well-ordered hearts requires a plan of action. We each need to choose a "rule of life," a practice that, when done regularly, will help us know Jesus and grow to be more like him.

1. Instead of telling his followers to have a balanced life, what did Jesus say is the quest worthy of our devotion? (See Matthew 6:33; 10:37–39.)

   SUGGESTED RESPONSE: *God knows that deep down we are looking for much more than just finding balance. Jesus calls us to pursue the kingdom of God above all else. We are to follow him with everything we have and to be willing to give up everything (even life itself) to follow him. This includes denying ourselves, which is quite different from pursuing life as we would like it to be.*

2. The apostle Paul was known not only for his devotion to Christ, but for his passionate appeals to other believers to pursue Christ. Note what he reveals about following Christ in the following passages.

[handwritten note:] City Slickers — Curly told Mitch to pursue the one thing that would truly make him happy.

SMALL GROUP EXPLORATION

The Quest for a Well-Ordered Heart

In Arthurian legend, people devoted themselves to the great quest for the Holy Grail, the ultimate symbol of communion with Christ. Today, the great quest of many people is for a "balanced lifestyle." But in God's kingdom, there is only one goal truly worthy of human devotion: pursuing a well-ordered heart. The transformation of our ordinary, fallen hearts into well-ordered hearts requires a plan of action. We each need to choose a "rule of life," a practice that, when done regularly, will help us know Jesus and grow to be more like him.

1. Instead of telling his followers to have a balanced life, what did Jesus say is the quest worthy of our devotion? (See Matthew 6:33; 10:37–39.)

2. The apostle Paul was known not only for his devotion to Christ, but for his passionate appeals to other believers to pursue Christ. Note what he reveals about following Christ in the following passages.

   a. To what did Paul compare his commitment to Christ in 1 Corinthians 9:25–27? In what way(s) does such a commitment nurture a well-ordered heart?

PLANNING NOTES

a. To what did Paul compare his commitment to Christ in 1 Corinthians 9:25–27? In what way(s) does such a commitment nurture a well-ordered heart?

SUGGESTED RESPONSE: *Paul compared the dedication needed to follow Christ to that of a competitive runner training to win a prize. He set his sights on something much higher than winning a mere race: his pursuit was eternal life with God. Paul had a purpose and was willing to make the sacrifice of discipline and training that was necessary to accomplish that goal. In a similar way, purpose, sacrifice, discipline, and training are necessary to nurture a well-ordered heart.*

b. What personal price was Paul willing to pay to accomplish his goal? (See 2 Corinthians 11:24–28.)

SUGGESTED RESPONSE: *Paul listed some of the suffering he experienced as a result of his devotion to Christ—shipwrecks, beatings, hunger, thirst, imprisonment, and much more. Obviously finding "balance" wasn't a high priority.*

3. What does Proverbs 4:23 reveal about the heart—the soul and spirit of our being? (See also Matthew 15:18.)

SUGGESTED RESPONSES: *We must guard the heart carefully because it is the "wellspring" of life. It is also the source of our thoughts and outward behavior.*

4. James 3:14–18 contrasts an ordered heart and a disordered heart. Note the source, characteristics, and fruit of each kind of heart.

Kind of heart:	Disordered heart	Ordered heart
Source	*Earthly, unspiritual, of the devil*	*Heaven*
Characteristics	*Bitter envy, selfish ambition*	*Pure, peace-loving, considerate, submissive, merciful, impartial, sincere*
Fruit	*Disorder and evil practices*	*Good fruit, a harvest of righteousness*

SMALL GROUP EXPLORATION

The Quest for a Well-Ordered Heart

In Arthurian legend, people devoted themselves to the great quest for the Holy Grail, the ultimate symbol of communion with Christ. Today, the great quest of many people is for a "balanced lifestyle." But in God's kingdom, there is only one goal truly worthy of human devotion: pursuing a well-ordered heart. The transformation of our ordinary, fallen hearts into well-ordered hearts requires a plan of action. We each need to choose a "rule of life," a practice that, when done regularly, will help us know Jesus and grow to be more like him.

1. Instead of telling his followers to have a balanced life, what did Jesus say is the quest worthy of our devotion? (See Matthew 6:33; 10:37–39.)

2. The apostle Paul was known not only for his devotion to Christ, but for his passionate appeals to other believers to pursue Christ. Note what he reveals about following Christ in the following passages.

   a. To what did Paul compare his commitment to Christ in 1 Corinthians 9:25–27? In what way(s) does such a commitment nurture a well-ordered heart?

   b. What personal price was Paul willing to pay to accomplish his goal? (See 2 Corinthians 11:24–28.)

3. What does Proverbs 4:23 reveal about the heart—the soul and spirit of our being? (See also Matthew 15:18.)

4. James 3:14–18 contrasts an ordered heart and a disordered heart. Note the source, characteristics, and fruit of each kind of heart.

Kind of heart:	Disordered heart	Ordered heart
Source		
Characteristics		
Fruit		

PLANNING NOTES

— 5. If we are serious about our quest for a well-ordered heart, we need to develop a "rule of life" or plan of action that will help us focus our daily activities toward that goal. The apostle Paul gave us two excellent examples that will help us know Jesus and learn to be more like him.

    a. Write down the "rule of life" found in 1 Corinthians 10:31.

       So whether you eat or drink or whatever you do, do it all for the glory of God.

    b. Write down the "rule of life" found in Colossians 3:17.

       And whatever you do, whether in word or deed, do it all in the name of the Lord Jesus, giving thanks to God the Father through him.

    c. Now write out your own "rule of life." You may use the Scripture passages above if you would like.

6. What will a well-ordered heart prepare us to do? (See Ephesians 5:1–2.)

    SUGGESTED RESPONSE: *To live a life of love, just as Jesus loved us and gave himself to be a sacrifice to God.*

Let participants know when one minute remains.

When time is up, ask the groups to rejoin as one group.

Group Discussion • *6 minutes*

Participant's Guide page 113.

As time permits, discuss the following questions that will help participants explore their understanding of the concepts covered during this session.

Now it's time for us to wrap up our discovery time. Please turn to page 113.

5. If we are serious about our quest for a well-ordered heart, we need to develop a "rule of life" or plan of action that will help us focus our daily activities toward that goal. The apostle Paul gave us two excellent examples that will help us know Jesus and learn to be more like him.

   a. Write down the "rule of life" found in 1 Corinthians 10:31.

   b. Write down the "rule of life" found in Colossians 3:17.

   c. Now write out your own "rule of life." You may use the Scripture passages above if you would like.

6. What will a well-ordered heart prepare us to do? (See Ephesians 5:1–2.)

GROUP DISCUSSION

1. Why is it so important for us to *intentionally* arrange our lives around the goal of spiritual transformation?

2. John Ortberg says that our problems with "balance" in life have more to do with internal disorder than with external disorder. In what ways do you think this is true?

3. We've explored the idea that a well-ordered heart leads us to love the right thing to the right degree in the right way with the right kind of love. What are some common pitfalls that hinder us from doing this? In which areas do you find this difficult to do?

PLANNING NOTES

1. Why is it so important for us to *intentionally* arrange our lives around the goal of spiritual transformation?

2. John Ortberg says that our problems with "balance" in life have more to do with internal disorder than with external disorder. In what ways do you think this is true?

3. We've explored the idea that a well-ordered heart leads us to love the right thing to the right degree in the right way with the right kind of love. What are some common pitfalls that hinder us from doing this? In which areas do you find this difficult to do?

4. When we think about spiritual transformation, we sometimes think about the "big" things we need to address. But a well-ordered heart takes into account everything, even the "little" things that are part of daily life. Let's look at the list of daily activities highlighted in the box below, and begin listing other things we need to be doing in Jesus' name. Consider how we would do these things differently if we did them in Jesus' name.

Living Life in Jesus' Name

- We could wake up in Jesus' name. When the alarm clock goes off, instead of thinking anxious or regretful thoughts we could rest in the assurance that God controls the day and sustains us!
- We could greet God first thing in the morning and invite him to go through the day with us.
- We could greet people in Jesus' name. We could notice them, look right at them, and listen to them.
- We could drive in Jesus' name — if we dared!
- We could watch television and movies in Jesus' name, not watching so much that it begins to create a disordered heart.
- We could do chores in Jesus' name, offering them as gifts to God.
- We could view our coworkers in Jesus' name — considering them to be valuable people, praying for them, being genuinely interested in their lives and families.
- We could spend money in Jesus' name.

GROUP DISCUSSION

1. Why is it so important for us to *intentionally* arrange our lives around the goal of spiritual transformation?

2. John Ortberg says that our problems with "balance" in life have more to do with internal disorder than with external disorder. In what ways do you think this is true?

3. We've explored the idea that a well-ordered heart leads us to love the right thing to the right degree in the right way with the right kind of love. What are some common pitfalls that hinder us from doing this? In which areas do you find this difficult to do?

4. When we think about spiritual transformation, we sometimes think about the "big" things we need to address. But a well-ordered heart takes into account everything, even the "little" things that are part of daily life. Let's look at the list of daily activities highlighted in the box below, and begin listing other things we need to be doing in Jesus' name. Consider how we would do these things differently if we did them in Jesus' name.

Living Life in Jesus' Name

- We could wake up in Jesus' name. When the alarm clock goes off, instead of thinking anxious or regretful thoughts we could rest in the assurance that God controls the day and sustains us!
- We could greet God first thing in the morning and invite him to go through the day with us.
- We could greet people in Jesus' name. We could notice them, look right at them, and listen to them.
- We could drive in Jesus' name — if we dared!
- We could watch television and movies in Jesus' name, not watching so much that it begins to create a disordered heart.
- We could do chores in Jesus' name, offering them as gifts to God.
- We could view our coworkers in Jesus' name — considering them to be valuable people, praying for them, being genuinely interested in their lives and families.
- We could spend money in Jesus' name.

PLANNING NOTES

PERSONAL JOURNEY: TO DO NOW

(**5** MINUTES)

Participant's Guide page 115.

Now let's turn to page 115 and spend a few minutes alone with God to review the key points and begin considering how what we've explored today makes a difference in our daily lives.

1. *Many of us desire a perfectly balanced, manageable life, but God wants us to pursue a much higher goal.* God wants to craft in each of us a well-ordered heart. A well-ordered heart seeks to follow Jesus and do what he would do. It loves the right thing to the right degree in the right way with the right kind of love. The pursuit of a well-ordered heart is worthy of our devotion, is achievable even in the most desperate situations, and produces good far beyond our sphere of influence.

   How seriously do you want to pursue life in the kingdom of God?

   Is pursuing God's kingdom truly the goal to which you have devoted your life? Why or why not?

   If Jesus were in your place right now, in what way(s) would his actions, words, and thoughts differ from yours?

2. *A well-ordered heart is a transformed heart.* If our ordinary, fallen hearts are to be transformed into hearts that love the right thing to the right degree in the right way with the right kind of love, we need a plan of action. That heart-changing plan of action consists of focusing the events of our daily lives around knowing Jesus and learning how to be more like him. It can be summarized by Paul's admonition in Colossians 3:17 to do everything in the name of Jesus.

   Write down your "rule of life" and memorize it.

PERSONAL JOURNEY: TO DO NOW

1. *Many of us desire a perfectly balanced, manageable life, but God wants us to pursue a much higher goal. God wants to craft in each of us a well-ordered heart. A well-ordered heart seeks to follow Jesus and do what he would do. It loves the right thing to the right degree in the right way with the right kind of love. The pursuit of a well-ordered heart is worthy of our devotion, is achievable even in the most desperate situations, and produces good far beyond our sphere of influence.*

How seriously do you want to pursue life in the kingdom of God?

Is pursuing God's kingdom truly the goal to which you have devoted your life? Why or why not?

If Jesus were in your place right now, in what way(s) would his actions, words, and thoughts differ from yours?

2. *A well-ordered heart is a transformed heart.* If our ordinary, fallen hearts are to be transformed into hearts that love the right thing to the right degree in the right way with the right kind of love, we need a plan of action. That heart-changing plan of action consists of focusing the events of our daily lives around knowing Jesus and learning how to be more like him. It can be summarized by Paul's admonition in Colossians 3:17 to do everything in the name of Jesus.

Write down your "rule of life" and memorize it.

Write down three daily activities to which you will begin to apply your rule of life.

Then put your rule of life into practice. Keep it in mind as you approach each event or interaction of your day. Focus on Jesus' presence with you, especially during these activities. Ask for his help or guidance in learning to be more like him if he were in your place. Or simply share with him what is on your heart.

PLANNING NOTES

Write down three daily activities to which you will begin to apply your rule of life.

Then put your rule of life into practice. Keep it in mind as you approach each event or interaction of your day. Focus on Jesus' presence with you, especially during these activities. Ask for his help or guidance in learning to be more like him if he were in your place. Or simply share with him what is on your heart.

3. *A well-ordered heart is perfected by faithful endurance through suffering.* God allows hardship and suffering in our lives to test our faith—to reveal our true values, commitments, and beliefs. God's testing is an act of love in that it refines, strengthens, and perfects our faith. Our perseverance through suffering produces character and makes our faith mature and complete so we can finish the race of life well. When we endure through faith, seeking to know God and to walk through our suffering in partnership with him, we discover a life of freedom, hope, and love—the life we've always wanted!

Think about the hardships and times of testing you have experienced. How do you typically respond to hardship?

In light of what you've learned during this session, how might you approach such times differently in the future? Or as you face a particular trial right now?

What is worth sacrificing or enduring in order to finish the race of life well?

What difference does it make to you that God wants you to walk through life—trials as well as good times—in partnership with him?

> Let participants know when there is one minute remaining.
>
> When time is up, encourage participants to continue the journey they have begun. Then end the session with the Closing Meditation.

2. *A well-ordered heart is a transformed heart.* If our ordinary, fallen hearts are to be transformed into hearts that love the right thing to the right degree in the right way with the right kind of love, we need a plan of action. That heart-changing plan of action consists of focusing the events of our daily lives around knowing Jesus and learning how to be more like him. It can be summarized by Paul's admonition in Colossians 3:17 to do everything in the name of Jesus.

Write down your "rule of life" and memorize it.

Write down three daily activities to which you will begin to apply your rule of life.

Then put your rule of life into practice. Keep it in mind as you approach each event or interaction of your day. Focus on Jesus' presence with you, especially during these activities. Ask for his help or guidance in learning to be more like him if he were in your place. Or simply share with him what is on your heart.

3. *A well-ordered heart is perfected by faithful endurance through suffering.* God allows hardship and suffering in our lives to test our faith—to reveal our true values, commitments, and beliefs. God's testing is an act of love in that it refines, strengthens, and perfects our faith. Our perseverance through suffering produces character and makes our faith mature and complete so we can finish the race of life well. When we endure through faith, seeking to know God and to walk through our suffering in partnership with him, we discover a life of freedom, hope, and love—the life we've always wanted!

Think about the hardships and times of testing you have experienced. How do you typically respond to hardship?

In light of what you've learned during this session, how might you approach such times differently in the future? Or as you face a particular trial right now?

What is worth sacrificing or enduring in order to finish the race of life well?

What difference does it make to you that God wants you to walk through life—trials as well as good times—in partnership with him?

PLANNING NOTES

CLOSING MEDITATION

(**1** MINUTE)

Dear God, so many things clamor for attention in our lives. It's tough to apply what we've learned today, to carve out time to develop a well-ordered heart, to commit ourselves to faithfully endure suffering. Now that we have a better understanding of what it means to pursue you and your kingdom above all else, help us as we seek to walk with you and do what you would do if you were in our place. You promise to guide us and help us, and we need your help. Thank you for the opportunity to partner with you in life. Guide us as we go out and do everything we do in your name, Jesus. Amen.

Old Testament Challenge

The Old Testament Challenge (OTC) is a turn-key program to help everyone in your church understand and apply the Old Testament. Participants experience the content in multiple contexts: through sermons, group discussions, and personal devotions.

This thirty-two-week series is designed for churches to teach, study, and discuss the entire Old Testament over a nine-month period. The goal of OTC is to discover the life-changing truths of the Old Testament and how they can be applied to daily life. Based on Pastor John Ortberg's OTC series at the New Community services of Willow Creek Community Church, this resource enables churches to raise the level of biblical literacy and understanding among their congregations. Your congregation will fall in love with the Old Testament!

The OTC curriculum is made up of four kits of seven to nine lessons each. This first kit covers the Pentateuch and includes everything you need to preach nine sermons (that's less than $25 per week!):

- Teaching Guide containing material from Ortberg's weekly teachings for pastors and/or teachers
- Group Discussion Guide focusing on specific passages from the Old Testament designed for weekly or bi-weekly use and including leader's notes
- DVD and VHS Video presenting an OTC "vision-casting" message from Ortberg, a promotional piece for churches, and four creative video elements for each kit to use during the OTC message
- CD-ROM providing seven to nine PowerPoint® presentations for use with each of the OTC messages. It also contains forty FAQ sheets answering tough questions from the Old Testament for use on your web site or to be printed in hard copy.
- Sets of slides for each teaching session for pastors and teachers
- Sermon Audio CD set containing all nine messages preached by John Ortberg
- Implementation Guide
- Taking the Old Testament Challenge reading guide

Old Testament Challenge –Kit 1: 0-310-24891-4

Old Testament Challenge –Kit 2: 0-310-24931-7

Old Testament Challenge –Kit 3: 0-310-25031-5

Old Testament Challenge –Kit 4: 0-310-25142-7

Pick up a copy today at your favorite bookstore!

ZONDERVAN™

GRAND RAPIDS, MICHIGAN 49530 USA

WWW.ZONDERVAN.COM

WILLOW

Willow Creek Resources

An Ordinary Day with Jesus

Experiencing the Reality of God in Your Everyday Life

This eight-session, ready-to-teach curriculum guides and equips both leaders and participants in concrete ways to embrace the very real person of Jesus Christ in everyday life

Christ entered our broken world to give us life in all its fullness. Not just in pinnacle experiences, but in every situation, every relationship, every activity. As you learn to recognize and welcome Christ's presence into every moment, ordinary days become filled with a tangible sense of God's presence. Suddenly, you are experiencing all of life with God—not just Sundays or "quiet times." Even more, he is transforming you in the process. You begin to experience the kind of ongoing, close connection to God you've longed for.

Take the first steps toward that kind of life today. *An Ordinary Day with Jesus* is designed to show you how. The practices and teaching detailed here can literally change your life, one ordinary-extraordinary-day at a time. Experiencing God's presence in your everyday life doesn't necessarily mean doing new things. It means doing the things you already do in new ways—with him. An ordinary day with Jesus truly can be the greatest day you've ever had. Best of all, it can lead to an extraordinary life!

The complete kit includes:
- Leader's Guide
- Participant's Guide
- 45-minute video cassette
- PowerPoint® CD-ROM

Kit: 0-310-24587-7

VHS Video: 0-310-24557-5

Leader's Guide: 0-310-24585-0

Participant's Guide: 0-310-24586-9

Pick up a copy today at your favorite bookstore!

ZONDERVAN™

GRAND RAPIDS, MICHIGAN 49530 USA

WWW.ZONDERVAN.COM

WILLOW

Willow Creek Resources

Good $ense

Transformational Stewardship for Today's Church

Are these the first words that come to mind when you think of stewardship? They could be! These are the words that people most often use to describe Good $ense—a field-tested, proven resource for changing hearts and lives in the area of finances.

Based on over sixteen years of ministry at Willow Creek Community Church, Good $ense by Dick Towner and the Good $ense Ministry team of Willow Creek includes resources designed to train and equip church leaders, volunteer counselors, and everyone in church.

- Church leaders—*The Good $ense Implementation Guide* and fifteen-minute *Casting a Vision for Good $ense* video equip church leaders to launch and lead a year-round stewardship ministry.
- Volunteer counselors—*The Good $ense Counselor Training Workshop Leader's Guide, Participant's Guide and Manual,* sixty-five minute video, and PowerPoint® CD-ROM train volunteers to become Good $ense budget counselors.
- Everyone in your church—*The Good $ense Budget Course Leader's Guide, Participant's Guide,* forty-five minute video, and PowerPoint® CD-ROM train every believer—not just those in financial difficulty—to integrate biblical principles into their lives both financially and spiritually.

At last, a resource that provides practical tools to address the challenging topic of finances in a grace-filled, life-giving way—a way that makes Good $ense.

Curriculum Kit: 0-7441-3724-1

Implementation Guide: 0-7441-3725-X

Vision Video VHS: 0-7441-3726-8

Budget Course Leader's Guide: 0-7441-3727-6

Budget Course Participant's Guide: 0-7441-3728-4

Budget Course Video VHS: 0-7441-3729-2

Budget Course PowerPoint® CD-Rom: 0-7441-3730-6

Counselor Training Workshop Leader's Guide: 0-7441-3731-4

Counselor Training Workshop Participant's Guide and Manual: 0-7441-3732-2

Counselor Training Workshop Video VHS: 0-7441-3733-0

Counselor Training Workshop PowerPoint® CD-Rom: 0-7441-3734-9

Pick up a copy today at your favorite bookstore!

ZONDERVAN™

GRAND RAPIDS, MICHIGAN 49530 USA

WWW.ZONDERVAN.COM

WILLOW

Willow Creek Resources

Everybody's Normal Till You Get to Know Them

John Ortberg

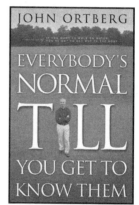

Not you, that's for sure! No one you've ever met, either. None of us are normal according to God's definition, and the closer we get to each other, the plainer that becomes.

Yet for all our quirks, sins, and jagged edges, we need each other. Community is more than just a word—it is one of our most fundamental requirements. So how do flawed, abnormal people such as ourselves master the forces that can drive us apart and come together in the life-changing relationships God designed us for?

In *Everybody's Normal Till You Get to Know Them*, teacher and bestselling author John Ortberg zooms in on the things that make community tick. You'll get a thought-provoking look at God's heart, at others, and at yourself. Even better, you'll gain wisdom and tools for drawing closer to others in powerful, impactful ways. With humor, insight, and a gift for storytelling, Ortberg shows how community pays tremendous dividends in happiness, health, support, and growth. It's where all of us weird, unwieldly people encounter God's love in tangible ways and discover the transforming power of being loved, accepted, and valued just the way we are.

Hardcover: 0-310-22864-6

Unabridged Audio Pages® CD: 0-310-25083-8

Unabridged Audio Pages® Cassette: 0-310-25082-X

Pick up a copy today at your favorite bookstore!

ZONDERVAN™

GRAND RAPIDS, MICHIGAN 49530 USA

WWW.ZONDERVAN.COM

If You Want to Walk on Water, You've Got to Get Out of the Boat

John Ortberg with Stephen and

Amanda Sorenson

"Lord, if it's you, tell me to come to you on the water."
—Simon Peter

Peter may have been the first one out of the boat, but Jesus' invitation to walk on water is for us all. But walk on water? What does that mean?

Walking on water means
- facing our fears and choosing not to let fear have the last word
- discovering and embracing the unique calling of God on our lives
- experiencing the power of God to accomplish what we would not be capable of doing on our own

This Zondervan*Groupware*™ helps you and your group answer Christ's call to greater faith, power-filled deeds, and a new way of knowing him. Relating the story in Matthew 14 to life today, teacher and bestselling author John Ortberg invites you to consider the incredible potential that awaits you outside your comfort zones. Out on the risky waters of faith, Jesus is waiting to meet you in ways that will change you forever, deepening your character and your trust in God. These six remarkable, interactive sessions will teach you how to discern God's call, transcend fear, risk faith, manage failure, and trust God.

What dormant gifts and dreams does God want to revive? What new visions does he want to kindle? What practical acts of obedience does he want to challenge you with? Discover the possibilities! Get to know Jesus as only a water-walker can, aligning yourselves with God's purposes for your lives. There's just one requirement:

If You Want to Walk on Water, You've Got to Get Out of the Boat

Sessions include:
1. What's Water-Walking?
2. The Tragedy of the Unopened Gift
3. Find Your Calling and Get Your Feet Wet!
4. Facing Our Challenges, Conquering Fears
5. Good News for Cave Dwellers
6. Learning to Wait on Our Big God

The complete kit includes:
1—90-minute VHS & DVD—use either format
1—Leader's Guide*
1—Participant's Guide*
1—*If You Want to Walk on Water, You've Got to Get Out of the Boat* hardcover book*
*Also sold separately

Zondervan*Groupware* delivers personal spiritual growth through:
- compelling biblical content
- minimal preparation time for both leader and participant
- proven learning techniques using individual participant's guides and a variety of media
- meaningful interaction in groups of any size, in any setting

Kit: 0-310-25053-6

Leader's Guide: 0-310-25055-2

Participant's Guide: 0-310-25056-0

Love Beyond Reason

Moving God's Love from Your Head to Your Heart

John Ortberg

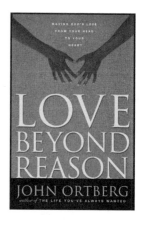

"Pandy" was only a child's rag doll—one arm missing, the stuffing pulled out of her. But in the eyes of the small girl who loved her, she was priceless.

In *Love Beyond Reason*, John Ortberg reveals the God you've longed to encounter—a Father head-over-heels in love with you, his child, and intensely committed to your highest joy. Ortberg takes you to the very core of God's being to discover a burning, passionate love that gives, and gives, and gives. He explores the life-changing ways this love has expressed itself through Jesus. And he shows how you, like Jesus, can love your mate, your family, your friends, and the world around you with the same practical transforming love.

Using powerful and moving illustrations Ortberg demonstrates the different characteristics of love—how it . . .

- hears the heart
- delights in giving second chances
- balances gentleness and firmness
- chooses the beloved
- touches the untouchable
- teaches with wisdom
- walks in grace
- searches for those in hiding

. . . and walks in the kind of humility that, in the person of Jesus, willingly descended from the heights to don the rags of our rag-doll humanity.

John Ortberg pulls back the curtains of misconception to reveal what you've always hoped and always known had to be true; God's love really is a *Love Beyond Reason*. And it's waiting to flood your life with a grace that can transform you and those around you.

Hardcover: 0-310-21215-4
Softcover: 0-310-23449-2

Pick up a copy today at your favorite bookstore!

ZZONDERVAN™

GRAND RAPIDS, MICHIGAN 49530 USA

WWW.ZONDERVAN.COM

  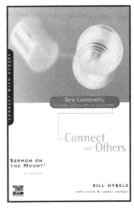 

Pursuing Spiritual Transformation

John Ortberg, Laurie Pederson, and Judson Poling

Experience a radical change in how you think and how you live. Forget about trying hard to be a better person. Welcome instead to the richly rewarding process of discovering and growing into the person God made you to be! Developed by Willow Creek Community Church as its core curriculum, this planned, progressive small group approach to spiritual maturity will help you:

• Become more like Jesus • Recapture the image of God in your life • Cultivate intimacy with God • Live your faith everywhere, all the time • Renew your zest for life

Leader's guide included!

Fully Devoted: Living Each Day in Jesus' Name: 0-310-22073-4

Grace: An Invitation to a Way of Life: 0-310-22074-2

Growth: Training vs. Trying: 0-310-22075-0

Groups: The Life-Giving Power of Community: 0-310-22076-9

Gifts: The Joy of Serving God: 0-310-22077-7

Giving: Unlocking the Heart of Good Stewardship: 0-310-22078-5

Pick up a copy today at your favorite bookstore!

ZONDERVAN™

GRAND RAPIDS, MICHIGAN 49530 USA

WWW.ZONDERVAN.COM

Willow Creek Association
Vision, Training, Resources for Prevailing Churches

This resource was created to serve you and to help you build a local church that prevails. It is just one of many ministry tools that are part of the Willow Creek Resources® line, published by the Willow Creek Association together with Zondervan.

The Willow Creek Association (WCA) was created in 1992 to serve a rapidly growing number of churches from across the denominational spectrum that are committed to helping unchurched people become fully devoted followers of Christ. Membership in the WCA now numbers over 10,000 Member Churches worldwide from more than ninety denominations.

The Willow Creek Association links like-minded Christian leaders with each other and with strategic vision, training, and resources in order to help them build prevailing churches designed to reach their redemptive potential. Here are some of the ways the WCA does that.

- **Prevailing Church Conference**—an annual two-and-a-half day event, held at Willow Creek Community Church in South Barrington, Illinois, to help pioneering church leaders raise up a volunteer core while discovering new and innovative ways to build prevailing churches that reach unchurched people.

- **Leadership Summit**—a once-a-year, two-and-a-half-day conference to envision and equip Christians with leadership gifts and responsibilities. Presented live at Willow Creek as well as via satellite broadcast to over sixty locations across North America, this event is designed to increase the leadership effectiveness of pastors, ministry staff, volunteer church leaders, and Christians in the marketplace.

- **Ministry-Specific Conferences**—throughout each year the WCA hosts a variety of conferences and training events—both at Willow Creek's main campus and offsite, across the U.S. and around the world—targeting church leaders in ministry-specific areas such as: evangelism, the arts, children, students, small groups, preaching and teaching, spiritual formation, spiritual gifts, raising up resources, etc.

- **Willow Creek Resources®**—to provide churches with trusted and field-tested ministry resources in such areas as leadership, evangelism, spiritual formation, spiritual gifts, small groups, stewardship, student ministry, children's ministry, the use of the arts—drama, media, contemporary music—and more. For additional information about Willow Creek Resources® call the Customer Service Center at 800-570-9812. Outside the U.S. call 847-765-0070.

- *WillowNet*—the WCA's Internet resource service, which provides access to hundreds of transcripts of Willow Creek messages, drama scripts, songs, videos, and multimedia tools. The system allows users to sort through these elements and download them for a fee. Visit us online at www.willowcreek.com.

- *WCA News*—a quarterly publication to inform you of the latest trends, resources, and information on WCA events from around the world.

- *Defining Moments*—a monthly audio journal for church leaders featuring Bill Hybels and other Christian leaders discussing probing issues to help you discover biblical principles and transferable strategies to maximize your church's redemptive potential.

- *The Exchange*—our online classified ads service to assist churches in recruiting key staff for ministry positions.

- **Member Benefits**—includes substantial discounts to WCA training events, a 20 percent discount on all Willow Creek Resources®, access to a Members-Only section on WillowNet, monthly communications, and more. Member Churches also receive special discounts and premier services through WCA's growing number of ministry partners—Select Service Providers.

For specific information about WCA membership, upcoming conferences, and other ministry services contact:

Willow Creek Association
P.O. Box 3188, Barrington, IL 60011-3188
Phone: 847-570-9812
Fax: 847-765-5046
www.willowcreek.com